'Along the Way'

SCENES FROM MY LIFE

BY

CAROL HAINES

BEARHEAD PUBLISHING

-BhP-

Brandenburg, Kentucky

www.bearheadpublishing.com

'Along the Way'

Scenes from my Life

by Carol Haines

Cover Design by Bearhead Publishing

First Printing - August 2017

ISBN: 978-1-937508-54-4

1 2 3 4 5 6 7 8 9

‘Along the Way’

SCENES FROM MY LIFE

INTRODUCTION

I have often wished that I knew more about my ancestors. Who were they? What was their childhood like? Who played with the worn, shabby dolls I found in my grandmother's cedar chest after she passed? Who wore the old-west-style, like-new, handmade dresses I found hanging in the back of her closet.

I wish I knew if my great-grandmother was truly one-quarter Cherokee Indian. Some of my great-uncles said she was, but she would never admit it. Now, I may never know for sure. And who was my husband's grandfather, who grew up in an orphanage in northern California? That, also, will remain a mystery.

So much history is lost from one generation to the next, unless, it is written down! This book is just that, a written history of events from my life. A glimpse of decades past for people my age to revisit, or for future generations who may wonder, like I do, what has been.

Writing this book has been an emotional experience for me. I have laughed, cried, and marveled at the journey that has been my life so far. I hope that you, dear reader, are entertained and amused as you travel along with me. Enjoy!

Chapter One

THE LUCKIEST GENERATION

My husband Mark and I were both wide-awake, staring into the darkness. *What should we do? Where will we go?* After discussing the offer from the Japan Air Lines pilot to lease our house for two years, we were no closer to a decision. Maybe the morning would bring an answer. It was June of 1987. We had moved to Anchorage, Alaska from California twelve years earlier. It was here we built a successful business, had our children, and made a good life. Now, that familiar, comfortable tapestry we had woven was coming apart at the seams. I settled back into my pillow and closed my eyes, wishing for a few hours of sleep in the hope of waking with a clearer mind. With a three-week-old baby and a three-year-old, a few hours were all I could hope for.

The following morning, I called my best friend Patti to get her advice. During our twelve years in Anchorage, Patti and her husband, Paul, had been just like family. They, too, were hit hard by the falling economy. Patti's company was relocating out of Alaska and she was offered a position in Oregon. I rocked the baby while I explained the details to her. "They have offered to lease our house for two years and the best part of the offer is Japan Air Lines will be paying the rent. It really is a great offer considering half of the houses in Anchorage are available, but there is a catch: His family will be arriving on Monday along with all their furniture and belongings. We will have to turn the house over to them in four days. He wants our answer today!"

Patti reassured me like she always did whenever I needed a sounding board. She said, "This is your opportunity to get out of Alaska if you plan to leave anytime in the near future. The movers from my company will be here tomorrow to get our furniture. If you agree I will send them to your place to get yours also. That way you will get your large pieces of furniture as far as Seattle with no effort on your part. You can pick it up there." Patti seemed to think we should accept the offer.

"Mark just walked in. I'll call you later and let you know."

When the price of oil plummeted in 1987, the oil-rich state of Alaska suddenly faced drastic cuts in revenue. Oil companies began laying off workers, and the economic boom the state had been enjoying became a devastating bust.

The perfect opportunity to leave the state had just landed in our laps. Should we accept? If so, how will we manage all that would be required in just a few days? On the other hand, later, we may look back and regret not accepting this unexpected offer.

I told Mark about Patti's offer, which put us under even more pressure to decide. It seemed that fate had bestowed its magic with the unlikely offer on our house, and Patti's plan to move our furniture. "If we accept Patti's offer, the furniture will be gone tomorrow, and we will have to be out before Monday. Where will we go?" I asked while my little Aaron nursed peacefully at my breast and his big brother looked from one parent to the other, sensing a shift in his idealistic world.

"Call your Mom," Mark said. "Your parents will be thrilled to have you and the boys stay with them while I wrap things up here. They have been dying to see their new grandson. I just spoke with Paul, and he said I could stay at his place since he is staying in town to finalize his business contracts while Patti goes on to Portland. I think we should take this opportunity to lease the house.

We'll figure out where we are going to resettle later. I have some opportunities to consider once I finalize our businesses here."

I called my parents before I took the boys upstairs for their afternoon nap, the last bit of normality in my soon-to-be-transformed life. Thank goodness our second-born son, Aaron, was a sleeper. He seemed to enjoy nothing more than his naps. Ryan and I tucked him in his crib, and we walked together, hand in hand, to Ryan's room. "Are we moving to Grandma's house, Mom?" he asked as his little lip trembled. I picked him up and told him we were going on an adventure starting at Grandma's and we would be together and safe. "I don't want to leave Alaska. I like it here."

"I know, pumpkin, but sometimes you have to be brave. If Mom and Dad hadn't been brave and come here, we never would have known how special Alaska is. We are lucky to have seen a part of the world most people never get to see. Can you be my helper because we are going to be very busy?" I laid him down and watched him cling to his security blanket as if it were his lifeline. I rubbed his back while looking around his room at all the things that made him feel secure and wondered if we were doing the right thing.

Just like that we were leaving the home we had lovingly built. The home built just for us, where everything suited us perfectly. Were we also about to lose the close friendships we had developed over the past twelve years, as well as the awesome views of the sparkling mountains that greeted me every morning, or the experience of being startled by a moose staring back at me when I opened the kitchen curtains? Would I ever pick blueberries in the midnight sun again, or share the excitement with everyone in town when word spread of the first salmon run of the season? Only time would answer these questions, but for now, I had to make good use of these nap-time hours.

Where to start? The furniture was to be picked up late the next morning, so I had to get it ready to go. With no time for boxes or suitcases, I started emptying drawers onto the floor, separating what we would take, and what we would temporarily store. I couldn't help getting emotional with our orderly world turning chaotic. I told myself that I had been thinking of moving closer to family for a while. Becoming reality, so suddenly, left no time to mentally prepare, and no time to mourn. My mind overflowed with questions and doubt. I had no doubt, however, that I would miss our beautiful, warm home. We had been so happy here, and the sadness of leaving it already tore at my heart.

The movers arrived on schedule and efficiently removed everything that made the house our home. There we stood among the clutter of what was left of our belongings: Piles of clothes on the floor, a few dishes and toiletries, and of course, diapers and baby necessities, and a sparse selection of Ryan's favorite toys. Our hearts felt as empty as the suddenly cavernous rooms. "Where are we going to sleep, Dad?" asked Ryan, rousing us from our thoughts.

"It will be like camping. We have foam mattresses and sleeping bags on the floor in our bedroom. Won't that be fun?" Ryan did not answer, but put the thumb of one hand in his mouth and grabbed onto my leg with the other.

That night, we all huddled together on the floor wondering what our future held. Money in the bank allowed us to be financially able to start over somewhere. I assumed it would be back in the San Francisco Bay Area where we grew up, and where our parents and childhood friends still lived. At least for the short term, that is where we planned to go, so I began to focus on being reunited with my relatives after twelve years of living so far away. It would be nice to spend time at Mom and Dad's, where they still treated me like their little girl. I could use a little loving care right now, and they loved their only grandchildren more than anything.

Mark helped us get settled on the airplane Sunday morning and kissed us goodbye. We had no idea how long we would be separated. Paul and he would be staying in Paul and Patti's emptied house, sleeping on the same foam pads that had been our beds the last three nights. I clung to the boys as Mark disappeared from our sight. A few months earlier, none of us could have imagined this upheaval of our predictable lives. I juggled the boys along with an assortment of snacks, toys, and an overflowing diaper bag in the confines of our two minuscule airline seats as we left everything we knew behind.

~

My old bedroom was exactly the same. Some of the furnishing had changed but all the memories of my youth still remained. I felt safe here, same as I did growing up. As expected, Mom and Dad relished having me home again; however, they were worried about our sudden departure from Alaska, where we had been so successful. The new baby and Ryan - the apple of Dad's eye - soon distracted them from wondering why we were there.

THE 50s

My family moved to this house in Concord, California, just east of San Francisco, soon after my first birthday. I lived there until I moved across town with my future husband. Our neighborhood was typical of 1950s America. The baby boom was in full swing, and every three-bedroom and one-bath house on the block was full of kids. The country had recovered from World War II, and none of us had heard of a far-away land called Vietnam. Our dads took the one car to work and our moms were always at home - usually in the kitchen, or in the yard hanging laundry on the clothesline, or having coffee with one of the neighbors. Mom was there to bandage skinned knees, make sandwiches and call us in when it got dark. I did not know one mother that worked outside the home.

Me on the front lawn of my childhood home in Concord, CA - 1955

My three siblings and I usually got along pretty well. I don't remember much rivalry between us. Jim and I, being the oldest, had the strongest bond. Tedd came along next, and even though he was born only eighteen months after me, we considered him the baby. He was small and fussy, demanding much of Mom's attention, so Jim and I learned to entertain each other. Then, my sister, Julia, joined the family two-and-a-half years later. Disneyland had opened two years earlier, and the Disney characters were already well known to us. A family friend took one look at the newborn Julie and said she looked like Tinkerbell. The nickname stuck, and she has been Tinker (at least to us) ever since. As adults we try to use her given name, but Tinker still slips out quite often. She was an adorable child and everyone who saw her commented on how pretty she was. Eventually she began to expect all the attention and praise. She was also a feisty little thing, especially when she didn't get her way - and that made her fun to tease. Jim used to love to tell her that she really wasn't pretty. She would turn red in the face, stomping her feet, shrieking, "I am too pretty!!!!!!" Boys can be so mean. Soon after my eleventh birthday, a third, unexpected brother, Jerry, joined the family. The four of us were enchanted with this new arrival. We adored him. When we arrived home from school, a chorus rang out: “I want to hold the baby first.” “No, I want to hold him first.” We each took a turn before we went on to our after-school playtime.

Jim, with Tedd on the rocking horse.
Me, driving the car, Christmas, 1955

The first vivid memory I have from my childhood is of my fourth birthday. I remember being excited, but a little shy about so much attention being paid to quiet, little me. My mother had made my birthday cake in the colors I requested, pink cake with purple frosting. It looked so yummy!

I remember sitting on our overstuffed brown couch, which swallowed me up, surrounded by balloons, as neighbors, young and old, arrived to celebrate my special day. My two closest friends, both named Kathy, one from next door and the other from across the street, marveled at my ruffled pink dress with the full skirt supported by layers of ruffled slips.

The neighborhood moms joined my mother in the kitchen for coffee and my friends and I examined what seemed to me a mountain of gifts, in reality only four or five. I don’t remember eating that beautiful cake or what was in the packages, but I remember that slightly overwhelming feeling of being the star of the day.

Dad was Catholic and Mom was a Baptist. Married in the Catholic Church, it was agreed that the children would be raised Catholic. Dad and all the kids went to church every Sunday morning, as most families did. Mom eventually converted so she could join us at Mass on Sundays, midnight Mass on Christmas Eve, and be with us as we received our First Communions and Confirmations. I did not attend Catholic school, but I did go to catechism twice a week. I always hated having to get up on Saturday mornings for catechism, while all the non-Catholic kids got to sleep in, and I will never forget the time my parents forgot to pick me up from catechism one Tuesday afternoon.

When I was little, I had a fear of being forgotten, or left somewhere. I started catechism in the first grade, and I was scared when dropped off alone, so far from home. Our elementary school was half a block from home, and we always went to church together. I was not used to being on my own. What if they forgot to come back and pick me up? On my first day, I got out of catechism, made my way out front with all the other kids, and to my horror I didn't see my parents' car. I told myself there were still a lot of kids waiting and they would be there soon. I watched anxiously for my parents to drive up as the number of kids waiting got smaller and smaller. *Where are they?* I worried. *How will I get home if they don't arrive soon?* Eventually I was the last child in the yard and there was not a soul in sight.

I began to cry, not knowing what else to do. Then I saw the door of the rectory across the street open, and the frightening, black-robed figure of Monsignor Hennessy step out onto the porch. As the gruff, no-nonsense priest spotted me, came down the stairs, and crossed towards me, in addition to crying, my small body shook.

"What's the matter? Why are you crying?" he asked in a caring manner.

"My parents forgot to pick me up from catechism, and I don't know what to do," I whimpered, wondering what he would do with me.

He reached down, took my hand and guided me back across the street to the rectory. He asked if I could tell him how to get to my house, and I told him I could. He told his receptionist to bring me out front while he went to the garage to get his car. I climbed in the back seat of his lengthy, luxurious (to me) car, and told him which way to go. When we drove up to the house, I saw Dad in the front yard mowing the lawn. He looked up as Monsignor pulled the car over to the curb. I jumped out of that car posthaste, racing into the house without as much as a nod of thanks. Oh, I was so happy to be home! I watched out the window as Dad went over to the car and talked to Monsignor. Embarrassed, he explained that he had gotten caught up in his yard work and lost track of time. When Mom heard what had happened, her comment was: "Why didn't you just walk home?" It had not occurred to me to walk home. I was only six-years-old for goodness sake, and the walk would have been about two miles. Parents had a different mind-set back then. But Mom's comment did not make me feel any better about this frightening experience.

~

On one salary, the budget was always tight, but we did not want for anything. Everything we needed was right outside: lots of kids to play with, our imaginations, and the freedom to explore the creek, the hills and anywhere else we could get to, and back, in a day's time. When the weather soured, we played board games or cards indoors or watched one of the three channels available on our black and white television - with rabbit ears that we moved around when the reception was bad. During these rainy days, trapped indoors, strong bonds formed with my siblings.

In the early part of the decade, we could not call a friend, because we had no telephone, not even a landline. If an out-of-town relative needed to contact us, they called our neighbors, the only family on the block with a phone, who would run to our house with the momentous news that we had a phone call! When my mother suggested we have one put in, my father asked, "What do we need a phone for? Who are we going to call?" It took my mother going into early labor in the middle of the night to demonstrate the benefits of having a phone to Dad. Soon after my new sister arrived home, a rotary dial phone was installed on the kitchen wall.

It was a great time to be a kid, even though we did not have many of today's conveniences such as having a pill for every ailment. Three of us four kids - until sibling number five came along much later - suffered from seasonal allergies, including hay fever and asthma. Somehow, Jim, the oldest, managed to escape this dreaded yearly ordeal. We were allergic to the blooming almond trees that grew in abundance around our neighborhood. Every spring we could count on itchy eyes, sneezing, and runny noses, soon to be followed by debilitating asthma.

No prescription drugs existed to help. We had to rely on over-the-counter antihistamines that knocked us out, as well as over-the-counter inhalers, which eased our asthma for all of five minutes, and could not be used again for three to four hours. As the season bloomed, we grew more and more listless. Soon we would be propped up in bed around the clock struggling for every breath. The weekend brought us blessed relief in the form of the coast. The ocean air cleared our lungs like magic, and we could breathe! Dad took us to the beach, the coastal redwoods, or into San Francisco to ride the cable cars and eat clam chowder at Fisherman's Wharf. We went to the zoo, museums, the Japanese Tea Garden, Chinatown, or anywhere the ocean breezes blew freely. We looked forward to our weekend excursions into the sea air because of the infinite opportunities to explore, discover, and breathe without effort. Even as a child, I remember the wonder of the giant redwoods, and loved hiking the trail through Muir Woods, with the coastal mist and pine scent filling my senses. And Dad had as much fun as we did.

Once the summer heat stifled the pollen, we were out the door, barefoot and carefree. We always returned home in time for dinner with the family, and then it was back outside to play hide-and-go-seek with all the neighborhood kids. Some nights we had camp outs in our backyard. Friends would stay over, and we would line up in our sleeping bags on our backs, counting shooting stars, telling scary stories, and watching for Sputnik, the mysterious Russian satellite that was launched in 1957, inaugurating the space age.

Once Tinker graduated from her crib in my parents' room, she moved in with me. We shared our small bedroom from then on. It was never a problem, and even though we had our own beds, while we were little we always slept together. As we got into our teenage years, the shared bedroom became much less cozy, but we still managed to make it work.

Jim, in the foreground.

Dad, Tedd, me and Julia on Mom's lap - 1959

Jerry, the youngest came along seven years later, much to everyone's surprise. A contented and happy baby, and he fit right in.

~

Christmas was a magical time at our house. My father was of German descent and I think Christmas traditions were a large part of his childhood, for he kept them alive for his family. Even though we did not receive many indulgences throughout the year, at Christmastime my parents pulled out all the stops. They put money in their "Christmas Club" savings account each week to make all our dreams come true for one enchanting time each year. We trimmed the tree with lights and tinsel and decked the halls with garland and wreaths. Together we baked cookies, made creamy fudge, and walnut-filled divinity candy. To add to the glow of our multi-colored holiday lighting, we crafted homemade candles in green, red, and blue. As my siblings and I counted down the days until Christmas Eve, we felt we might burst with excitement.

The oldest of the five, even though he was three years older, my big brother, Jim, and I had an especially close relationship. As the activities concluded one Christmas Eve, begrudgingly, we kids were sent off to bed. My sister fell fast asleep, just as she always did, and I lay awake anticipating what treasures awaited us come morning.

"Sis, Sis, are you awake?" It was my brother peeking in to see if I was as restless as he was. "I think I hear Mom and Dad putting our presents under the tree," he whispered. We were pretty young, but I don't remember ever believing in Santa Claus. A realist, I always knew Mom and Dad played Santa. A gas heater, located in the wall between the bedrooms and the living room, kept our cozy house warm. Slats in the upper part of the heater allowed a view into the living room. We stealthily crept up to the heater and peered through the slats to see what goodies were being unveiled.

We stood in the warmth of the heater, holding hands, quiet as two church mice, as we watched until the last gifts were tenderly placed around the tree to insure maximum impact on Christmas morning. Suddenly it was time for us to rush back to our beds to avoid being caught in the act.

Even though we had been up so late, my brother and I were the first ones up in the morning. Despite our secret preview, a lot of surprises still awaited us. I am not sure why I remember that Christmas Eve so clearly after all these years. Maybe because I was young enough still to feel completely sheltered and safe.

~

As the seasons changed so did our family activities. In addition to our springtime weekends at the coast and our traditional holiday celebrations, Dad, being a lover of nature, had us camping all summer. We even camped at the beach in the winter occasionally, or took day trips to the Sierra Nevada when the snow was falling. The annual road trip back "home" to Oklahoma, where my parents grew up, was our major vacation. Each year, in the heat of July or August, we loaded up the car (six people, no air-conditioning) and headed south to the historic Route 66, which we followed across the deserts of the Southwest. Despite how torturous this sounds, I looked forward to the adventure and beauty of the desert experience. We started out each day hours before daylight and stopped early in the afternoon to escape the extreme heat reflecting off the highway in waves. Dad went to bed as soon as we got checked in to our accommodations, and Mom took us out to the hotel pool where we cooled off and burned pent-up energy. We all retired early in preparation for a 3:30 a.m. wake-up call. When the call came, we sleepwalked to the car with the promise we would stop for breakfast later. While Mom and my siblings settled in for a few more hours of sleep, Dad and I enjoyed the cool solitude of driving the long straight road with nothing but millions of stars to keep us company.

I sat behind Dad in the backseat, watching the shimmers of moonlight on the sand and the ghostly tumbleweeds bouncing by, all the while watching the horizon for signs of dawn. These quiet mornings, crossing the desert at sunrise, while my siblings slept, brought me a feeling of peace and calm during the sun's silent awakening, first appearing as a pale pink light in the distance. Soon the sky and softly rolling dunes began to change from silvery black to blue, lightened with hints of pink and purple. As the sun rose, with it came shades of orange, red, and finally, bright, clear light, and the heat of the day was soon upon us.

For this trip, Dad reasoned it a good idea to fill the glove compartment with candy and gum to keep us quiet during the long, hot, stretches of driving. I would chew a stick of gum until the flavor disappeared and then reach up to throw it out Dad's rolled-down window. Sometimes the gum stuck to the car door right below Dad's window, where it would melt in the searing sun. Eventually Dad would place his bent arm out the window, directly on the sticky gum mess, causing it to stick to the boiling hot car door. It made him furious to have to pull over and attempt to remove the gum both from the car, and his hairy arm. We, on the other hand, thought this was the funniest thing ever.

During our roadside rest stops, we would dash out among the odd-shaped cacti to search for unusual rocks, plants, and - in my older brother's case - creepy crawlers. He would inevitably return with some desert creature he had captured: A hairy spider, scaly lizard, or a spiky horny toad. Thankfully these creatures were not usually allowed in the car, but occasionally Jim would smuggle one in to terrify me when he got bored. And he was frequently bored.

Once we reached our destination, Grandma's house in Tecumseh, Oklahoma, new adventures abounded. For kids from the San Francisco suburbs, small-town country life was paradise. We had sleepovers with our numerous cousins, went to the swimming hole, or lake to water ski, or just outside to climb trees and learn about different plants, bugs and animals. Jim learned a hard lesson about skunks. After a skunk sprayed him, he got quarantined outside to sleep on a cot until the smell finally went away.

Taken in front of Mom's childhood home in Tecumseh, OK - 1960

While in Oklahoma, I was introduced to my Native American ancestry. On my dad's side we are members of the US Government-recognized Citizen Potowatomi Nation, whose reservation is in Shawnee, Oklahoma, not far from Tecumseh. On my mother's side, we are Cherokee. Unfortunately, her family would not admit to being Native American because of prejudice, so I am not legally recognized as a Cherokee.

Each summer, the Potowatomi held their annual Pow Wow. This event was not like the organized, commercial Pow Wows we know today. Once when I was very little, Dad took some of us to the Pow Wow, which was being held outside of town. I remember walking through high reeds or stalks of some kind, feeling anxious and small, eventually emerging in a clearing where a large bonfire blazed. I watched wide-eyed as the natives danced their traditional dances to the beat of drums. Not in fancy costumes, they wore very little (all males as I remember), with feathers on their heads, paint on their faces, and they shook crude instruments. For a small child to witness, the scene appeared very wild and frightening. Soon my fear dissipated as I watched the dancers, lost in their movement and song. Their skin glistened in the firelight and their long feathers and beads swayed rhythmically, hypnotizing me with wonder. I have kept that image with me all these years and remember this glimpse of my tribe's last days of living traditionally, as a moment in history.

If it hadn't been for the yearly trip back "home," I might never have gotten to know, or maybe even met, all of my wonderful cousins. We had such fun together as kids, and I must say, as adults, they are some of the best people I have ever known. They are still a lot of fun too! I am very grateful to have known my grandparents, and aunts and uncles as well. I love hearing stories about when my grandmother pulled her younger siblings out of their burning house, when she purchased the first car in town, or when she worked full time as a legal secretary, supporting most of the family through the Depression. Stories about my uncles hopping on the outside of moving trains when traveling to Arizona for work picking oranges, and hanging on with their bare hands, which came close to freezing off during an ice storm. The lives they led differ so greatly from our lives today, being somehow more real. Yes, they worked harder physically, but they did not have the burden of technology. The stories of their struggles and achievements leave me a vision of a richer, more rewarding life.

~

There was never a dull moment when my brother Jim was around. Even when he wasn't around, Mom and I worried about him. He had no fear and would do almost anything. One summer he became fascinated with snakes, collecting them during his daily ventures to wherever boys went once school was out. The collection was relegated to the garage, but this did not stop Jim from sneaking some of them into his bedroom. One evening after dinner, the family went visiting, and upon our return Jim meekly asked Mom if she would get mad if he told her something. "Well, I don't know if I will get mad until I know what it is you are going to tell me," Mom replied. With Jim you just never knew.

"You have to promise you won't get mad or I won't tell you," Jim bargained.

"I can't promise but you better tell me because you know I will find out sooner or later," Mom exclaimed, getting a little irritated.

"Well, I had three of my snakes in my room when we left… and now there is only one."

"What do you mean there is only one?" Mom asked, with her eyes as big as saucers.

"I had a piece of cardboard over the top of their terrarium. They must have pushed it off and got out."

Soon the news spread throughout the family and the panic set in, especially among us females - and the search began. We looked under every piece of furniture, in every cupboard, and even in our shoes. There was no way we were going to bed with two snakes slithering around the house. I did not want to wake up with a snake in bed with me.

The snakes were never found, and I opened every drawer and closet door with trepidation for weeks after their great escape. Jim's only regret was that he lost two of his favorite snakes. Mom, with her limitless supply of patience, took Jim's antics in stride, rarely losing her cool.

Our camping trips in the Sierras allowed him the freedom to hike, swim, fish, or attempt any number of activities during which he would disappear with a new friend from a neighboring camp for the entire day. I, being more cautious, fretted that he was at the bottom of the river or lost in the forest, but just as night began darkening the trails, he would emerge from the cover of the pines with tales of his discoveries and adventures to tell around the campfire. We usually camped with our close friends who had five children, so with our four, and a friend or two thrown in, there would be close to a dozen kids. What could be more perfect? These camp outs were pure freedom for us kids. We swam in the freezing cold river, picked buckets full of wild blackberries, and slept soundly in the crisp mountain air.

Duty-bound for his great love of the outdoors, Dad shared this passion with his children. When camping in national forests and parks, he would sign us up for walks and talks with the rangers. When camping at Yosemite, which was not yet overrun with tourists, at sundown he would round all the kids up and take us to the park garbage dump, where we could watch the bears climbing around, foraging for food. Never left disappointed, the bears always showed up. Later in the evening, we would find a vantage point from which we had an open view of a magnificent wall of granite, watching the "fire fall" of hot coals come cascading down its face. The coals were pushed over the edge of Glacier Point strategically, to appear as a waterfall of fire, which is exactly what it was. Even for children this was a spectacular sight. We watched with our heads tilted back and our mouths hanging open. This spectacle ended in 1968 when someone decided that it caused too much congestion in the park, and that spectators were trampling the meadows. I don't know how many people are still alive that witnessed this historic tradition. My dad made sure I was one of them.

Unlike my siblings, I was always willing and ready to accompany Dad on the ranger walks or listen to their educational talks. They looked so official in their brown uniforms with their smoky-the-bear hats, and, I respected their knowledge of my Sierra Mountains, which I loved being in: The flora and fauna, the adventure of hiking and exploring, eating Dad's fabulous camping breakfasts, stargazing, and the nightly campfire. The two moms would find a large granite rock and put it in the fire until it became white-hot. After allowing it to cool slightly, they would put the rock at the bottom of their sleeping bags to warm their feet through the cold mountain nights. They claimed it worked great until the night Jean's rock caught her sleeping bag on fire.

After the campfire died down each night, we all retired to our tent and sleeping bags with the old flimsy, blow-up air mattresses that constantly went flat. Dad's handy-dandy repair kit patched the leaks for maybe half a night. My siblings and I woke on many mornings lying on the cold hard ground and knew the patches had failed again. It didn't bother us too much. We would jump up, put on our sweatshirts, and rush out to warm ourselves by the fire that dad would have roaring. The smell of bacon frying, mingling with the crisp pine-scented morning air, with the campfire warming my back, is, to this day, one of my all-time favorite memories.

Roomy enough for all of us, we six slept in one giant tent. Our canvas shelter had one unique feature that made it stand out among all other tents. It was pink. This fact is a never-ending joke in our family, and we still laugh about it today. We can only guess that Dad got a good deal on it. Unfortunately, I don't have a picture of the pink tent, but I do have many fond memories - the night it blew down on us in gale force winds while camping on an island in the delta, or the year the spiders wanted to make it their home, and we had to inspect every inch of it each night before bed to make sure all the spiders were out. I could actually see the spiders in the dark and would wake everyone, screaming: "There's a spider on my sleeping bag!" - And there was.

~

Before we knew it, fall arrived, and that meant back to school. During the summer between second and third grade, I experienced a growth spurt. When trying on last year's school clothes, I discovered I had outgrown most of them. "MOM!" I called out, "When are we going shopping for school clothes?"

"Soon," - she responded. "But you will only be getting two dresses." We wore only dresses. Pants on girls were unheard of. "And one pair of shoes. The boys need school clothes also, and our budget is limited."

How could I start the school year with only two new dresses? I wondered. Two dresses just weren't enough, but I didn't know what I could do about it. Then I had an idea. We had a sewing machine, and typical at the time, I had watched Mom do mending and some sewing. *I could learn to sew my own clothes!* I calculated that the money for the two new dresses would buy enough fabric for at least four or five. If Mom would agree to help me get started, I could have a new wardrobe.

I took my plan to my parents, and they thought it was a great idea. Dad stated that he would buy me all the fabric I wanted, if I learned how to sew. Mom took me shopping, and we purchased fabrics and patterns that she felt I could master at my age. Her lessons consisted of showing me how to lay the pattern on the fabric, cut the pieces out, and read the instructions on how to sew them together. That really was all the guidance I needed. I found the directions comprehensive, and by the end of the third grade I was making all of my clothes. I became a competent seamstress, and enjoyed creating my own clothes as well as occasionally making clothes for Mom, which she loved.

All the neighborhood kids walked to and from our elementary school each day, which was right down the street from our house. I usually walked with one of my *best* friends, Kathy from across the street with her freckles and curly red hair, who was always in some sort of trouble with her mom, or Patricia who had the same birthday as me, a fact that we felt bonded us as *special* friends. With so many kids on our street, friends always surrounded us.

We studied together, played together, and grew up together. I am still friends with some of my old neighbors and have known them as long as I have known my siblings. At my parents 50th wedding anniversary party in 2000, a couple who still lived around the corner from my family home reminded me of their son, my old classmate, with this story I had long forgotten.

Already hot, towards the end of the school year, the entire school was out on the playground for the annual track competition. My girlfriends and I were not paying much attention to the contests, but the guys all excitedly waiting for their turns. A group of boys hung around the coach, who held the stopwatch, timing the runners as they ran the 50-yard dash. They watched each runner and anxiously waited to hear the time. I was unaware, that Michael, the son of the couple now telling the story, had just set a new school record and remained on pins and needles hoping that no one clocked a quicker time. When they called for the girls to run, the boys still watched, to make sure Michael's record would stand. My name was called eventually, and I positioned myself at the starting line. I had no expectations, I just planned to do my best and hope for a good grade in PE. When the timer sounded, I ran with everything I had for that short fifty yards. As I caught my breath and heading over to the coach to get my time, I noticed the sudden quietness, and everyone stared at me with their mouths hanging open. I had no idea what was wrong, and wondered if something was showing that shouldn't be. Upon reaching both the coach and Michael, I found them checking and rechecking the stopwatch. To Michael's dismay, I had beaten his time! He had just lost the title of fastest runner in the school. And to his shame, he had lost it to a girl! I don't remember being proud or excited, just feeling sorry for crushing Michael's excitement.

Michael's parents told me that he went on to become a college track star with many California collegiate titles to his record. However, he never lived down the humiliation of my stealing his thunder all those years ago. I told them I would be willing to meet him for a rematch, but I have yet to hear from him.

~

One summer the family did not take the annual trip across the scorching desert to Grandma's house. Instead, my parents announced that Tedd, my next youngest brother, and I would be traveling on our own, by airplane no less, to spend the summer at Grandma Rosie's and Grandpa Harvey's. I was thirteen at the time, and Tedd was eleven, almost twelve. We were really excited to be taking this trip on our own and looked forward to spending the summer with our cousins, catching fireflies, swimming at the lake, and climbing trees.

Our first time flying on an airliner, we boarded the Western Airlines (The Champagne Airlines) flight in San Francisco. For two middle class kids from the suburbs, this experience alone offered a major adventure. How flying has changed since that time: Dressed up people, good food, and an overall refined experience. The pretty and friendly, flight attendants in their caps and uniforms helped Tedd and I get settled. We felt very grown up and somehow special as we looked down at the tops of the clouds below us. We landed in Oklahoma City and our grandparents met us. Soon we settled in our own rooms at the familiar house where our mom had grown up.

Grandma Rosie's youngest brother, Uncle Junior, and his wife, Aunt LaVera, had two kids: Iris, who was two years older than I was, and Joe, who was about Tedd's age. They were our partners in crime for the entire summer. Iris and I were inseparable, as were Tedd and Joe. Uncle Junior worked on the Santa Fe Railroad, and would be gone for a few days, and then home for a few days. He also had a boat, and on his days off, we packed our bathing suits and the six of us drove to Lake Thunderbird, where we set up a camp-site and spent the days water skiing, fishing, exploring, and enjoying the lake, where there may or may not have been any other campers or boaters. The memorable summer ended all too soon.

For our trip home, Grandma and Grandpa combined our transportation with an opportunity to visit their only daughter. We packed our belongings, said a tearful goodbye to our cousins, and climbed into Grandpa's thankfully air-conditioned car for another journey on the now historic Route 66 through the desert states of Texas, New Mexico, Arizona, and finally into California. The drive had so far been uneventful as we crossed the mountains through Flagstaff, Arizona, and once again found ourselves on the desert floor. As the hot afternoon dragged on, Grandma startled us by exclaiming "Harvey, Harvey, are you all right?"

He didn't respond, and suddenly alert, we registered the panic on Grandma's face. Grandpa gripped the steering wheel, stared straight ahead, and did not respond to our questions, or move at all. We continued down the highway at about sixty miles an hour with an unresponsive driver. Luckily the road was as straight as an arrow, and by quick thinking Grandma reached over and turned off the ignition. She took hold of the steering wheel and guided us to the side of the road.

Beside ourselves, Tedd and I wondered what was happening, but Grandma must have realized that Grandpa had had a stroke, and we managed to get him in the back, semi-reclined on the seat, with me by his side. Grandma jumped behind the wheel and drove like lightning, focused on getting us to the nearest town. I could feel my heart pounding in my chest as I prayed that Grandpa wouldn't die before we reached help.

Grandpa responded to my carressing his brow as we covered the empty miles, eventually arriving in a small, dusty, desert town. Amazingly there was a small hospital in the town, and we went straight there. Grandpa was admitted, and Tedd and I were left in the waiting room for the longest time wondering what would happen next.

When Grandma finally emerged to find us, she explained to us that Grandpa indeed had had a stroke, and would be in the hospital indefinitely. "Is he going to be all right?" we wanted to know.

"He is very sick. The doctor thinks he will recover, but he doesn't know how long it will take. Let's go get you something to eat, and find a hotel." Naturally Tedd and I worried about Grandpa, but being pre-teens, we worried more about ourselves. We found a motel and Grandma just - left us there, in a sparse, adobe style room furnished with two twin beds and a small desk and chair. We just looked at each other, wondering what we would do in this lonely place indefinitely.

The next morning, we took the money Grandma had left us and ventured out on our own into the dry hot day, looking for breakfast. In the course of about twenty minutes, we discovered a couple of restaurants, a couple of stores, the hospital, and absolutely nothing else remotely interesting. Each day we walked from one end of town to the other, visited Grandpa at the hospital, ate meals at one of the restaurants, and tried to stay positive. After a few days of this monotonous routine, and no date for Grandpa's release in sight, the welcome news came that we would be rescued.

Mom and our oldest brother, Jim, who had just gotten his driver's license, drove down from the Bay Area. Mom stayed in Arizona to be with her parents during this crisis, and Jim drove Tedd and me home. Once on the road, I worried about Jim's limited driving experience, but he did just fine and I was delighted to be getting out of that seemingly lifeless, hot, dry excuse for a town.

After another week or two, Mom and my grandparents arrived home. Grandpa was doing pretty well, and he did recover from most of the damage caused by the stroke. They stayed with us for quite awhile and returned home when they felt comfortable with Grandpa's health.

~

The 1950s were a peaceful, rebuilding time. My parents, along with most others I knew, worked hard and enjoyed the fruits of their labors. On any given Saturday, the dads were outside mowing the lawn or washing the car, while the kids rode their bikes or skated on roller skates, and Mom, as usual, was in the kitchen or doing laundry. As the decade ended, and we entered the 1960s, life as we knew it was about to change.

THE 60s

Most adults and some teenagers smoked cigarettes, and at some point during the early 60s the adults in my world all started drinking cocktails. All of a sudden my parents, and all their responsible hardworking friends, became party animals. Was it because their kids weren't babies anymore, and the breadwinners' jobs were secure and stable by this time? I am not sure, but the times, they were a-changin. Shag carpet and olive green or harvest gold appliances were being installed in homes across the country. All females had big, ratted, stiffly sprayed hair. My friends and I sat in front of our vanity mirrors with a tall can of Aquanet hair spray perfecting our personal big hair looks. Along with the big hair we wore miniskirts and the classic white go-go boots, made popular by Nancy Sinatra, and her hit song, THESE BOOTS ARE MADE FOR WALKIN'.

After working hours, every adult I knew had a cocktail in one hand and a cigarette in the other. On Friday and Saturday nights, our thirty-something parents dressed up and went out to socialize, leaving the kids home with the oldest sibling or a neighborhood teenager in charge. I babysat my infant brother at eleven years old - a thought that horrifies me today. I know that my parents' generation did a lot of drinking and driving during this time, but everything seemed to turn out okay. I don't remember hearing about DUI's until later. In many cases, including my father's and some of his friends, the drinking eventually got a little out of hand.

~

In 1960 the country elected John F. Kennedy, the youngest man ever to hold the office of President. The young and handsome Kennedys moved into the White House with their two adorable little children, bringing optimism and hope to the entire country. Two years later, Kennedy, along with the entire country, looked World War III right in the face.

The Cold War had been chilling between the United States and the Soviet Union since the end of World War II. People built bomb shelters in their yards, and all the neighborhood kids gathered to watch one being built around the corner from our street. The world feared Soviet aggression in Europe. At the same time, the United States and Russia competed for supremacy in technology, the space race, and military might. In October of 1962 they came to a frigid standoff, when the United States discovered Soviet ballistic missiles, capable of launching nuclear warheads, on the communist island of Cuba. These warheads could have reached several major US cities. I was only nine years old at the time and did not understand that my secure world was on the brink of destruction. I do remember my parents literally sitting on the edge of their seats, watching the news and President Kennedy's speech to the American people that struck fear throughout the country. World War II was very fresh in my parents' minds, and they knew how close we were to an even more catastrophic, nuclear war. I briefly wondered what was so riveting on the news that afternoon, but was still innocent enough to believe my parents would always keep us safe, and ran outside to join the neighborhood kids for a game of hide-and-go-seek.

The United States positioned a blockade of ships to meet the approaching Soviet ships as the country watched their TVs on pins and needles. By the grace of God, the Soviets backed off, and the crisis was over. America breathed a sigh of relief, but the Soviet leader, Nikita Khrushchev, remained public enemy number one.

Kennedy's popularity rose after the Cuban Missile Crisis and the population was enchanted with their charismatic first family. Then, on November 22, 1963, tragedy struck. An ordinary day in my 5th grade classroom, the principal's voice came over the "loud speaker," which is what we called the intercom, announcing that President Kennedy had been shot and killed. Even as ten-and eleven-year-olds, we felt a devastating loss, and upon arriving home that afternoon I found my mother in tears as she watched the news. A veil of sadness covered the country.

Families gathered around their television sets for days, watching the procession of mourners pass by Kennedy's flag-draped coffin as he lay in state. We watched three-year-old John Kennedy, Jr. salute his father's casket on its way to the cemetery, a sight that brought a tear to almost every eye, including mine. We had loved our charismatic president, and the country said a sad goodbye together.

Me standing next to the boys wrestling coach, 1967.
Apparently white knee socks were all the rage.

~

In the heart of the emerging drug culture, living in the San Francisco Bay Area, I was more of an observer than a participant. While our parents enjoyed their social lives, their kids were being introduced to marijuana, seconal (reds), barbiturates (beans), and any number of recreational drugs becoming popular in our high schools and colleges. Even though I was always ready for an adventure, I wanted at the same time to be in control, so I was very cautious regarding drugs and alcohol. Having experienced childhood asthma, I wanted nothing to do with cigarettes. I appreciated breathing too much.

In the late 60's, when I began high school, the peace-loving, mind-blowing, hippie culture really blossomed. Our big, ratted hair was now long and straight, and not just for girls. The Beatles appearance on The Ed Sullivan Show introduced the idea of long hair for males to American kids, creating intense friction between the hippies and their World War II veteran fathers. Our war-hero fathers hated the long, shaggy hair and tie-dye clothes their sons wore, but the movement was too powerful to hold back.

The neighborhood gathering place, my friends met at our house because my older brother and his friends congregated there, and vice versa. Mom welcomed all the neighborhood kids who met at our house every morning. She shuttled us all to school, and we assembled there again in the afternoons. There were some long term matches made at our house, including a couple of marriages.

In addition to experimenting with miscellaneous drugs, some of my peers celebrated free love (sex), as well as LSD and cocaine. I, personally, did not want to deal with the consequences of "free love" and the harder recreational drugs, so I stayed on the sidelines. The third part of the 60s drugs, sex, and rock and roll culture - the music! - I did not shy away from.

I was not officially allowed to date as a high school freshman except when it came to school functions, but that rule was easy enough to get around. The exploding Bay Area music scene was expanding all the way out to the suburbs, including our bedroom community of Concord. We went in groups to hear as yet unheard of groups like Santana and Sly and the Family Stone. I remember driving by the Concord Armory, which was being used for community events, in a car loaded with friends, seeing a banner announcing "SANTANA – Sat night at 8:00 p.m." Most of us had not heard of Santana, but someone had heard they were supposed to be really good. Needless to say, seeing the great Santana in this small, local venue was unforgettable. I became fascinated with the magic artists can create on their guitars, and, have always been drawn to the soulful masters, George Harrison, Eric Clapton, Jimmy Page and Jimi Hendrix, to name a few. Little did I know at the time that later in life I would have a new guitar hero, my son, Aaron. As fabulous as these artists are, they could never thrill me the way Aaron does when I watch him on stage with the guitar we bought him years ago. It amazes me how good he is getting.

Sonny and Cher also played in Concord during my freshman year of high school. They must have been in a career slump to be performing in the suburbs, but we enjoyed seeing the already famous couple singing all of their hit songs.

One of my brother's friends took me to my first major rock concert in 1967, the summer of love, to see the Chambers Brothers. This first experience at the Fillmore West in San Francisco was allowed because it was Steve's sister's birthday, and he was taking her boyfriend and her as his gift to her. Steve invited me, and Mom agreed that I could be part of this birthday celebration. For me the experience was a celebration of life - the soulful music, the psychedelic colored light show, the beautiful people - and I was hooked.

If Mom had known what Bay Area rock concerts were like, marijuana smoke filling the air, and bottles of wine laced with LSD being passed around, I would have missed seeing some of the greatest bands of all time. But she didn't know, and for the next few years I went to concerts most weekends. Led Zeppelin, Janis Joplin, Aretha Franklin, Credence Clearwater Revival, Jimi Hendrix, Jefferson Airplane, the Rolling Stones, Eric Clapton, Crosby, Stills & Nash, the Animals, Elton John, and on and on. Regretfully there are a few of the greats that I missed due to circumstances beyond my control (my mother wouldn't let me go), most notably, the

Beatles (I was a little too young), the Who (who actually played in Concord also), and the Doors. If I had it to do over again, I would have found a way to get to these shows. My friends and I took for granted that great bands were playing every weekend in and around San Francisco, not appreciating that we lived at the heart of a legendary music scene that would eventually come to an end. I am grateful that I grew up in the right place at the right time to experience this era of rock and roll, because I have not seen or heard anything that compares since.

By this time everyone knew about that far-away place called Vietnam. When the draft started in 1969, our brothers and friends received draft notices and got shipped overseas to face the horrors of war. Little option remained if your number came up, unless you had a disability or wanted to go live in Canada for the duration. Mark, who would become my husband, missed the draft by one number, and my older brother was spared also. But many of our friends went, and some of them did not come home. The ones that did come home were not the same innocent kids they were when they left.

~

I was a member of a tight little group of girlfriends throughout high school, and some of us are still friends today. We have started a tradition of getting together each year for a weekend to catch up, visit, drink wine and laugh about old times. And we did have some great times growing up together. The group consisted of a couple of wild, do-anything girls, a couple of fun lovers who went about it more sensibly (I was among this group), and our group mom, Shelley. Shelley was always worried we would get caught, be late, or get hurt. We would laugh at her and call her Mom when she tried to rein us in, but in the end, she went right along with the rest of us.

Very close friends, we went on vacations with each other's families, had slumber parties staying up all night eating junk food, cut school just to see if we could get away with it, and came in from the pool together on a warm summer evening to watch Neil Armstrong and Buzz Aldrin make the first footprints on the moon, on July 21, 1969.

Not the prettiest of girls, Shelley, our group mom, shocked us when she turned up pregnant in our junior year of high school. Shelley, the cautious one who worried about everything; really? But first love is a powerful force to be reckoned with, and she was unprepared when it stuck her. Greg was her first boyfriend, and they were inseparable. Even though it was 1969 and the woman's movement had already begun, there was really no question as to what would happen. Shelley dropped out of school and married Greg. Months later baby boy Michael was born and all was well. The rest of us carried on as usual, visiting Shelley on occasion. She seemed content and very much in love. We thought they would live happily ever after, but it was not to be.

As Memorial Day weekend approached, word was going around that there was going to be a gigantic party at Yosemite Valley over the long weekend. Of course my group just had to be there. We tried to persuade Shelley and Greg to join us, but they were moving to a new place, and wanted to use the three days to get settled in their new home. Hundreds if not thousands of young people from the Bay Area descended on Yosemite Valley, overrunning the unsuspecting families and tourists that were camping there. Needless to say it was a fantastic weekend of partying in one of the most spectacular settings on earth. I had a great time, but I do regret the havoc we wrought on the park that weekend.

We rode home Monday night in the back of a friend's van and were dropped off to find our parents waiting with mournful expressions on their faces. Shelley had died. My parents knew that I had been close to Shelley, and they relayed the details of the freak accident as compassionately as they could. For some reason that I still don't understand, Greg and Shelley kept a loaded gun high on a shelf in a closet of their home. As Greg packed for the move, he brought the gun down with the other articles on the shelf and the gun went off. Greg was in the hall and Shelley was in the living room, but somehow the bullet found Shelley's chest and killed her almost instantly. In our youthful innocence, and having no experience with death, we were all stunned.

Greg was not charged with any crimes and Shelley's death was ruled a tragic accident. I did not know Greg all that well personally, but at the time, I never doubted his innocence.

That spring we laid our friend to rest and learned that life could be dangerous and sometimes unfair, and that it goes on no matter our individual traumas. I also realized that I was very lucky to have loving and nurturing parents who got me through my first loss.

~

My siblings and I, along with most of our friends, survived the 60s, and by the 1970s the baby boom generation matured into young adults. Our neighborhood was blue-collar and few of us were guided towards college. We assumed after graduation we would find a job, leave home, get married, and have kids. The young female population planned to continue working even after becoming mothers, not quite realizing we were aspiring to two full-time jobs.

Late in my senior year, one of my close friends introduced me to her boyfriend's close friend, Mark. He will tell you that we had already met, but I don't remember this first meeting (apparently he didn't make much of an impression). Mark had a "chopper," a motorcycle with an extended front end, and asked me if I wanted to go riding the following Saturday. I agreed, and he told me he would pick me up at noon. After completing my Saturday morning chores, I grabbed my jacket and watched out the front window for Mark to arrive. My mother asked where I was going, and I explained that I was going riding with my new friend, Mark. About that time, he drove by the house on his extremely chopped motorcycle, in his riding leathers, with his long hair flying. My mother's eyes just about popped out of her head.

"You are not going out with THAT, are you?"

"Oh, Mom," I exclaimed. "He is really nice. You will like him when you meet him."

Mark and I soon became an item as we realized we had so much in common, mainly our love for the great outdoors. He grew up camping with his family, just as I had with mine. Also an avid fisherman, together with his fishing buddy, he brought in fresh fish each weekend, which I very much appreciated. I encouraged him to try snow skiing, and even though he hesitated, he gave it a try. To my delight, after a few times out, he was up to speed with me, and soon, to my dismay, he surpassed my skill level. He was (and still is) a natural on the slopes.

After graduation, while still living at home, my older brother, Jim, returned home after a failed attempt at supporting himself. We were still close, and he approved of Mark being in my life. It was during this last time which our family would be together in our home that tragedy once again marked my life.

~

I remember the warmth of one August night as Jim and I drove through town in his unmistakable, blue-panel truck. It was evident to me that night that almost everyone in town knew that truck and its owner. We were both hanging around the house that summer night and had decided to catch the latest hit comedy. Friends and acquaintances waved and shouted greetings to us as we pulled up to the speaker at the drive-in movies. As the last of the evening light softened to a dusky purple, we mingled outside our vehicles waiting for darkness to signal show time.

Jim's life-loving attitude and infectious laughter were especially irresistible that night. By the end of the movie our sides ached, but that didn't stop us from giggling all the way home. Once I changed into my pajamas and climbed into bed the security of family and home soothed me off to sleep. At the time I didn't realize I would cherish the memory of this last outing with Jim for the rest of my life.

A few nights later I was roused from my contented sleep by my parents' voices and got up to find them fumbling with their jackets and keys, looking confused and disconnected. "Where are you going?" I asked.

"We're going to St Francis Hospital. Jim has been in an accident and has been taken to the burn center there, and we have to get to him!" *Burn center,* I thought, *Oh my God!* Too distressed to verbalize the questions forming in my mind, I stood helplessly as they rushed out the door.

They drove off leaving me standing in the doorway shivering against a chill that wasn't there. I went to check on my six-year-old brother who slept obliviously, as were my teenage brother and sister. Up until now, our childhood had been ideal. Nothing bad had happened within our immediate family. With one phone call I felt our sheltered world changing, and fear rose inside me. I considered waking Julie, but decided we should both rest in preparation for what I suspected would be a stressful day. I trembled as I pulled up the blanket, and envied Julie's peaceful sleep.

Images and scenarios invaded my restless mind as I imagined the worst for my big brother. *Is he in pain? Is he burned? Is he going to die?* Then a vision of my mother and father, driving through the darkness, distraught and anxious, brought the reality of the situation home. My hardworking, ever-present, unconditionally loving parents had left here looking like helpless, lost children. I had never seen them so shaken, and the security and innocence of my youth dimmed as a new maturity dawned.

Mom and Dad returned home about 9:00 in the morning looking drained and heartsick. They told us Jim had been badly burned in the car accident. He had been a passenger in a pickup truck, which had been run off the road, then rolled over and burst into flames. He was in critical condition and might not make it. It took a few seconds to sink in that my worst fears were now reality. Grief and despair encompassed us as my tearful gaze took in the five sorrowful faces surrounding me. Then I thought of Jim, in the hospital, alone and scared, and a surge of adrenalin rushed through me. I began to take charge and make decisions. Mom would stay home and rest, my sister would look after little Jerry, and I would drive Dad back to the hospital. And so our sad journey began with me taking the lead. My plan was simple and instinctual. My own need to receive comfort was no longer the priority, replaced by the drive to give comfort to my parents and siblings. Overnight I had crossed the threshold from childhood into a more serious adult world.

Days turned into weeks of going back and forth to the hospital. Mom and Dad went most days, while I took care of the household responsibilities. At eighteen I had not cooked much, but I had been around the kitchen enough to figure it out. The meals I prepared were pretty basic, spaghetti, or fish sticks, but during these bleak days we all had knots in our stomachs that didn't leave much room for food anyway.

When Mom and Dad returned home in the evenings, listless and broken from the agony of watching their son suffering, we knew there would be no encouraging news, but only more descriptions of the horror of the burn center. I ached with worry as I watched my family weakening and did my best to remain positive and supportive. Caring for them made me feel strong and kept me going. Much of my time passed with my little brother, answering his questions as best I could. He seemed to understand that Jim was hurt and that Mom and Dad had to be with him. We read his storybooks and played games. He was very well behaved, sensing the seriousness of the situation.

Knowing that death could come to our big brother at any moment, my teenage siblings and I began to alternate trips to the hospital, relieving one parent at a time. It was good to be with Jim, but heart wrenching to see his condition. The pain, constant, the morphine induced hallucinations that frightened and confused him. "Hey Sis" he managed to say when he saw me there. I managed to keep a smile on my face while I filled him in on happenings around the neighborhood, even as he cried out in pain. My parents' unwavering love and devotion to Jim kept them going, but I think we were all unconsciously prepared for the worst.

Weeks turned into months and Jim clung to life. Setbacks shot down brief glimmers of hope. The doctors still did not know if he would pull through - and if he did, the road to recovery would be long and difficult, with surgeries, skin grafting and therapy.

Driving home from the hospital with my mother after what had been an unbearably heartbreaking day, I struggled to maintain my composure when I looked over at her and glimpsed her steadiness and calmness. I marveled at her strength and courage, and I wondered if she were fighting her emotions to protect me. I felt sure that she was, and warmed with love and respect for her. At that moment I vowed I would remain strong and carry as much of this sorrow as I could for her and my dad.

That night in bed, while praying for God to relieve my brother from the endless pain and suffering, the shocking realization came over me that I was praying for Jim to die. No, I didn't want him to die, but I didn't want him to continue to suffer, and death really was the only relief for him. I no longer knew what I should be praying for and longed for my innocent, less-adult life.

With heavy hearts, we settled into a routine of hospital visits and struggling to get through the days and nights. After three months of this agonizing ordeal we progressed through the motions of living, but were numb to everything but worry. The doctors had warned us a couple of times that Jim was failing, but then he would stabilize again. The hospital called very early one gloomy morning in November, requesting that my parents come over right away, as they feared they were losing him. We kids waited at home for the news we instinctively knew was coming.

My parents drove home later that morning, and we watched through the window as they got out of the car and walked toward us. There was a sense of relief or acceptance in their carriage, definitely a change in their posture. My heart tightened as I summoned what strength remained there. Jim had died not long after they arrived. He went peacefully and his pain and agony were finally over. I had never seen Dad shed tears until that fateful day as he spoke of our loss and we all cried together. Despite our sadness, I felt a sense of peace surround us, a lightening of our burden, and relief for Jim.

Now my parents faced the most difficult of life's challenges, burying their child. My mother was exhausted and knew she could now rest. I soothed her as best I could and kept everyone fed and functioning, while my dad, with the help of family and friends, took care of the last arrangements and decisions he would ever make for his son. To this day I don't know how he managed to get through the process. Maybe he wanted to be sure everything was as good as it possibly could be for his firstborn.

After the relatives went back home, and the flowers had all been thrown out, we drifted back into our previous routines, and the slow process of healing began. The glaring absence of the larger-than-life figure that was my brother was difficult to avoid, but we tried to fill that empty space with happy memories and funny stories. As time went on, it got easier.

The unspoken change in the relationship I shared with my parents was not so glaring but nonetheless very real. My parents were still my parents, but something had shifted in me. Older and stronger, I now realized that life was unsure. I had learned to cope, learned to help, and learned to be an adult.

~

Since high school I had kept a part time job at the mall, scooping ice cream. After Jim passed away I took a job at Stretch and Sew. The nationwide company sold knit fabrics and taught classes on how to sew with them. With the sewing skills I had taught myself as a child, I was the star of the store. I did it all: Sold fabric, taught classes, all the while modeling their patterns. At the same time, I identified a career path to pursue, which started at a local business school. The school was preparing their students for jobs with the newly relocated computer center for Chevron (Standard Oil at the time) right there in our hometown. I took the courses and was immediately hired to work in the Master Records department at Standard Oil, just a couple of miles from my home. This was probably the best job I could have secured within our local community. Before Standard Oil moved to town, most jobs required a commute into San Francisco. The working conditions were excellent and I spent my days keeping the customer files updated - address changes mostly, thousands of them, day after day. Even though I did well and fit in - making friends, and joining groups - I eventually realized I might not be cut out for this strictly structured work environment. Punching in and out, and my production being carefully monitored, went against my free-spirited nature.

Meanwhile, Mark had joined the Carpenters Apprenticeship Program. In those days carpenters actually had to learn the trade in the classroom as well as on the job. He worked full time and attended classes a couple of evenings a week. While we got our careers going, Mark's widowed mother planned to get remarried. She had a condo that she was eager to sell and offered Mark a deal he couldn't refuse. We decided to purchase this nicely appointed townhouse and move in together. My parents had a hard time at first with the relatively new concept of living together before marriage. But soon they realized that we were going to be together and they accepted us as a couple from then on.

Mark's father had lost his life a few years before I met him. Once he told me the story of how his dad died, I remembered having heard about it on the local news. His dad had been a captain with our local fire department, and his engine had been involved in a tragic accident that made the front page of the local news. On the way to a call, upon entering an intersection, a gravel truck struck the engine, snapping Mark's father's seatbelt and throwing him to his death. The entire community mourned the loss of this upstanding family man, and seventeen-year-old Mark, along with his mother and two younger brothers, had to learn to cope with their own life changing loss.

Chapter Two

YOUNG, MARRIED, AND LOOKING FOR ADVENTURE

The United States economy was struggling during the 1970s. The country grew increasingly weary of the Vietnam War, interest rates skyrocketed, and the OPEC, (Organization of Petroleum Exporting Counties), oil embargo, refused to sell oil to allies of Israel, causing us to wait in long lines for hours to get gas for our cars - sometimes only to be turned away once we reached the pumps because the day's allotment was gone.

Despite the economic challenges of the time, Mark and I were thriving. We both were making good money, and being from modest means, we were used to budgeting and living frugally. Our savings account grew and we enjoyed an active social life with friends and family. Mark's fishing buddy, Jim, and his wife, Denise, were our closest friends, and we went out to eat all over the Bay Area, when we were not at home in our condominium in Concord, preparing the fresh catch of the week. Jim and Denise also enjoyed camping, and we went to the mountains with them just as we had with our families. However, as summer turned to winter, we could not persuade them to try skiing. A three hour drive for us, we loved spending our winter weekends at the ski resorts of the Sierras.

Life was good, and we began to feel the pressure from some of our family (Mark's Italian grandmother) about getting married.

"I will be dead before I see a grandchild from you." She could lay a guilt trip like nobody's business. I loved her to death. The classic Italian matriarch, oh how she could cook. Her cooking weighed heavily in my decision to marry into this family. I must have been Italian in a past life because I have always been drawn to the Italian culture.

February 15, 1975, we tied the knot; having a big family wedding in the Catholic church we had both grown up in. No wedding planners in those days, I planned the entire event myself. I also planned to make my wedding gown, but I waited too long to get started. As luck would have it, I found and bought my dream gown, which fit perfectly, right off the rack. A slim fitting A-line silhouette of ivory lace over silk. My gown had a high neckline and long sleeves, typical for wedding dresses at that time. Mom, who had taken cake decorating classes, created a four tiered wedding cake and with the help of Mark's mother and grandmother, we prepared much of the food for the reception ourselves. The day was warm and sunny and we danced well into the night. For our honeymoon we headed off to Utah for a week of skiing.

The happy bride, February 15, 1975

The happy couple

~

One morning, after a bright, sunny weekend on the slopes of Heavenly Valley at beautiful Lake Tahoe, I returned to work with "raccoon eyes", the mask left from being sunburned everywhere on my face except where my sunglasses protected it. As I sat down across from my co-worker, we looked at each other and broke out laughing. She had the same "raccoon eyes," and we knew that we shared similar memories of a fabulous weekend of skiing.

Connie and I had just begun working together, and on our break we shared our common interest in skiing and the great outdoors in general. We became fast friends, and out of the blue she suggested Mark and I join her and her husband, Mike, at their friends' cabin the following weekend. I told her that sounded great, but we didn't know these people and couldn't just show up announcing we had come there for the weekend.

"Yes you can," she explained. "If you ski you are welcome. The policy at Tom and Doris's cabin is the more the merrier." But I wasn't sure.

Connie invited us over for dinner to meet her husband, Mike, who proceeded to encourage us to join them on their ski weekends at Tom and Doris's South Lake Tahoe cabin. As it turned out Tom and Doris were the parents of Mike's best friend. Tom, together with his sons and any friends they could enlist, built the Tahoe cabin (actually a nice house) over the course of a couple of years. Mike had joined the construction crew on most weekends until it was completed. His reward was a key to the cabin and an open invitation, of which he made good use.

Despite their age difference, Tom and Doris being our parents' age, the two couples equaled in their abilities on, and love for, the ski slopes. Tom and Mike were exceptional skiers, and Doris and Connie were a level or two below. The group skied together until the guys broke away to conquer the challenging double black diamond runs. Mike and Connie were convinced that we would fit in perfectly. Even though we had not yet met Tom and Doris, we decided to accept their invitation and join them the following weekend.

Mike and Connie were able to get an early start that Friday afternoon as Mike was still in college. He picked Connie up right after work. We were to follow later. Highway 50, which leaves the freeway at Sacramento, eventually turns to a winding, two-lane pass over Echo Summit, before dropping down to South Lake Tahoe. This route gets very treacherous on Friday evenings when many Bay Area and Sacramento Valley residents are leaving the workweek behind, looking for excitement and adventure in the casinos and on the ski slopes, especially if it happens to be snowing.

Mark and I did not get on the road until about 6:30 p.m., which would put us in South Shore about 10:00 p.m., best-case scenario. Unfortunately, this night would not be a best-case situation. It had begun to rain in the Bay Area earlier that afternoon and the forecast was for heavy snow in the Sierras. A winter storm warning does not stop skiers, right? This is what we hope for. We were well equipped with Mark's 4-wheel drive truck, cold weather gear, and youthful abandon, while our new friends and host and hostess anxiously awaited our arrival.

As soon as we began to ascend the foothills east of Sacramento, the rain began to stick to the windshield in chunks of sleet and ice. The visibility was poor, and the traffic bogged down. We crept along turning up the heater and defroster while the windshield wipers smeared the slush around, offering intermittent views of the worsening conditions and the "CHAINS REQUIRED AHEAD" signs. Excited to be starting our weekend, this challenge of getting over Echo Summit during a storm provided an extra adventure before we even arrived in Tahoe.

This being sunny California, folks headed into these treacherous driving conditions with street tires on their sedans, hoping they would not be required to "chain up." However, on that night weekenders would need all the help they could get. Skittish drivers began to pull over and attach their chains before they found themselves in trouble. We felt secure with our all-weather tires and the 4-wheel drive engaged.

For the next three hours we snaked up the mountain in bumper-to-bumper traffic, passing spun-out cars stuck in snowdrifts, while the wet, miserable owners tried to free them. At last we reached the summit amidst howling winds and snow that piled up before our eyes. Visions of the Donner Party, who, in 1846 had been stranded at the top of these mountains in their covered wagons and forced to resort to cannibalism to survive, flashed through my mind while we slowly followed the faint glow of taillights ahead, when suddenly, Bam! We were pushed forward, almost ramming the car in front of us. We had been hit from behind.

Mark jumped out and found a brand new Saab with its front-end smashed into the back of our truck. The driver and two passengers thankfully were unhurt, but the car was totaled. In the midst of the blizzard, with the traffic stalled behind us, we managed to push the car to the edge of the very narrow two-lane road. The three stranded girls grabbed their bags and the driver hopped into the cab with me, while the others dove into the unheated shell on the back of our truck. Mark slammed the tailgate and rushed into the cab bringing a flurry of snow and steam with him. The five of us began the treacherous descent into the valley, abandoning the Saab precariously perched just off the road. Oh well, it was totaled anyway.

Our new traveling companion explained that it was her birthday and that a friend had lent her his brand new car to bring to Tahoe. Poor guy, I have no idea what became of his car. As we made our way down from the summit, the raging storm and the traffic eased off a little, and we regained our composure. We dropped the girls at a hotel making sure they had enough money and a plan to be rescued. By now it was 3:30 in the morning, and we were exhausted and so ready for a warm bed. Reading our directions with a flashlight, we maneuvered the truck through the unplowed side streets of South Lake Tahoe finally arriving at what we hoped was the right place.

With our bags over our shoulders, we trudged up the snow-laden steps to the front of Tom and Doris's house. Not wanting to wake the entire household, we peered through a crack in the blinds and saw that Mike and Connie slept on the sofa bed just a few feet from us on the other side of the window. In luck, we proceeded to tap on the window. Tap, tap…tap, tap, tap. No response. "Mike, Connie, wake up, let us in! No movement. Tap, tap... knock, knock, "Wake up… They can't hear us, knock louder." KNOCK, KNOCK, "WAKE UP IN THERE, WE ARE FREEZING OUT HERE!" As we looked in on them all snuggly and warm in their bed the door suddenly burst open. We stared up to see a disheveled, scowling, Tom (or so we assumed), glaring at us from inside. "We're Mike and Connie's friends," we stammered. "We were trying to…"

Tom cut us off.

"Just come in and keep the racket down!" he growled, and lumbered back down the hall.

By then Mike and Connie finally awoke and laughed at our concern that we should go to a hotel after the impression we must have left on our hosts. They assured us all would be forgiven come morning and showed us to our room. We settled under our goose down comforter appreciating the lovely accommodations, but anxious about our next encounter with Tom.

Over breakfast the next morning we described the storm and our mishaps crossing the summit to our captive audience. They were highly entertained and amused, all the while offering sympathy. Afterwards the guys went out to have a look at the back of our truck. The damage was minimal, and we loaded up for a day on the slopes. The storm over, the air sparkled with frosty light, and the six of us formed friendships that day that lasted for years. For the rest of that winter and the next, we spent every weekend at the Lake Tahoe cabin, skiing, hot tubing, grilling steaks in the fireplace, and bonding. It could not have been more perfect. After the last traces of snow disappeared from the slopes, we overloaded our backpacks - including frozen steaks, potatoes for baking in our campfire, and bottles of vodka - and struck out to a destination pinpointed on a forest service map. Our outings always included adventure, excitement, laughter, and the best sort of companionship.

Tom, Doris, Mark and I. Aspen, Colorado, 1977

One weekend our destination was Grouse Lake, sitting at 9,300 feet, deep within the Mokelumne Wilderness Area. The long, strenuous hike was grueling with our overloaded packs, but we arrived at the lake well before dark. After setting up camp, we built a fire, made cocktails, and soon realized our exhaustion from the hike and the thin air at that altitude. As we relaxed by the fire, someone noticed a sign attached to a nearby tree. It was a warning to beware of bears that were known to be in the area and also advised backpackers to string all food items high in a tree away from their camp at night. We had already planned to do that after we consumed some of our food supply at dinner.

We baked our potatoes and grilled our steaks while enjoying the views, the companionship, and the cocktails. I was thinking about getting ready for bed when we remembered we had to get the food put up for the night. By this time the guys were feeling the effects of the day, the altitude, and the alcohol.

The girls got the food wrapped and tied with netting and turned it over to Mark, Tom, and Mike to find a tree away from our tents. It was dark by then, and the hunt for the perfect tree was on. After shining flashlights all over the forest, a tree was chosen with a high branch out of any bear's reach. "I'll throw the rope over the branch, tie the food with the rope and we will hoist it up," Tom explained. It took them about an hour to get this simple task accomplished as they laughed for ten minutes after each failed attempt. You would have thought you were watching an episode of The Three Stooges instead of three grown men. Their laughter echoed through the pines and probably scared any bears within fifty miles of us away. The food was finally secured and the show was over. The times we spent together as a group of fun lovers remain some of my most cherished memories. Our time together was not long enough.

Mark, Tom, Doris, Connie, Mike. Grouse Lake, 1975

~

When Mike graduated, the economy was still limping along and jobs were in short supply. His father (upper management with Chevron in Anchorage, AK) came through with a great offer for Mike. However, there was a catch. The position was in Alaska, where the economy was booming with the discovery of the Prudoe Bay oil fields, and the construction of the pipeline to transport the oil from the top of the world, down the length of Alaska, to the Port of Valdez. Mike and Connie had expected this offer, but for the rest of us, it was devastating. What would we do without our perky, smiling, energetic Connie, and our more serious (before cocktail hour) college student? But the handwriting was on the wall. We were about to lose a crucial third of our whole.

After Mike and Connie left, nothing was the same, or as much fun. They called us regularly, excitedly describing the Alaskan landscape, the midday darkness, the Northern Lights, a boomtown bursting at the seams, and jobs for all. "No ski report yet due to the darkness, but we are ice skating, snow machining, and making tons of money. You should come up."

It sounded like the ultimate adventure; and a little seed was imbedded in our minds.

~

The six of us were never to be together again. In addition to weekends at Lake Tahoe, Mark and I took a few memorable ski trips with Tom and Doris to Colorado, Utah, and Wyoming over the next few years; however, when we started having babies, we stopped jetting off on ski vacations, so time and distance kept us from seeing each other. We always remained in touch and we grieved when our dear friend Tom fell seriously ill. An excellent skier, even at 75 years old, Tom was head of the ski patrol at his local ski resort, which allowed him to ski everyday. Suddenly, he started to fall while skiing. Tom never fell, so he knew something was very wrong. Test results confirmed Lou Gehrig's disease, which took his life a short while later. I am so glad we knew him. He taught us how important it is to live life to the fullest.

Chapter Three

EGGS ARE A DOLLAR APIECE

Mark had been an avid fisherman for most of his life, and Alaska was the sportsman's ultimate destination. Going there had never crossed our young minds, but now that our good friends were there, our imaginations ran rampant. We began to discuss the merits of joining Mike and Connie, and found more positives than negatives. *Are we nuts to consider it, or is it a fabulous opportunity?* Both of us felt the draw of the North.

While we went about our daily lives, not thrilled with my position at Standard Oil, I began daydreaming about the wildness of Alaska. I had a good paying job, close to home, but I recognized that I did not fit well into the corporate environment. The rigid structure, the rules and regulations, all went against my free-spirited nature. Each day the lure of the last frontier became stronger and stronger. Having grown up being exposed to nature's beauty, the prospect of moving to Alaska sparked my curiosity. By this time Mark had completed his apprenticeship, and was a card-carrying member of the Carpenters' Union - was it time for change? We had been saving money, didn't plan to start a family for a while, and knew that once we did, we would have to put family first. With each passing day we felt more sure we were destined to follow our hearts and go north.

GOING TO ALASKA

"Alaska, are you out of your minds? It is so expensive up there; I hear eggs are a dollar apiece! You have jobs, a home, why would you leave?" My father, the nature lover, expressed his distress with claims that we knew to be exaggerations. The rest of the family had similar concerns, and even our friends thought it an outlandish plan. Despite this resistance, or maybe because of it, our decision to head north became final. We would give it a year and then probably return home to our condominium. In our youthful innocence, (or ignorance), the plan was simple. Quit our jobs, rent out our condo, store our furnishings, load the truck, and drive the Alaska Highway (of which seventeen hundred miles were unpaved in 1976) in February. Mike and Connie, in their exuberance over us joining them, sent us a copy of the Milepost, a mile-by-mile guide of the Highway. Even though they had flown to Anchorage, they relayed to us that it was the general consensus among the locals that winter was the optimal time to drive the unpaved Alaska Highway, citing packed snow and ice to be less problematic than dirt, dust, and mud, which sounded logical to us - we did have our 4-wheel drive vehicle, after all. In reality, we had no idea what was in store for us.

DRIVING THE ALASKA-CANADA HIGHWAY

Once the truck was loaded with everything we felt we needed, all of our outdoor gear, work clothes, a giant bag of homemade cookies Noni, Mark's Italian grandma presented to us, and the Milepost, we said our tearful goodbyes to family and friends. Even though everyone expressed their concern, I think some envied our bold decision. We estimated we would be on the road about a week, having mapped out our route with our trusty Milepost, planning to overnight at the recommended towns along the highway. The first leg of our journey was as expected. We stopped in Washington State to visit a friend and then on to Vancouver, British Columbia where we took a side trip to Whistler Mountain to do some skiing. From Vancouver our route took us into the interior of beautiful British Columbia where the tall evergreens with their frosty tips stood in clusters surrounded by blankets of deep, white snow.

As we drove along munching on Noni's cookies, a bright sky and a clear road greeted us. We made good time and figured to be at the day's destination, Fort St. John, around dinnertime. With each passing mile we could feel the temperature dropping. We adjusted the heater as needed while the daylight faded. By the time we reached Fort St. John, night had fallen as we pulled into a service station to refuel before finding our lodging for the night. Mark opened his door and a burst of frigid air penetrated right through my layers of sweaters. *Wow, we were not in California anymore!* He struggled with the iced-over gas cap and couldn't wait to get back inside. Slapping his gloved hands together and fogging up the windows with his breath, we faced cold like we had not experienced before.

The clerk at the motel told us it was somewhere around 30 degrees below zero and bound to get colder through the night. He gave us our key and directed us to our room. We climbed an exposed stairway to reach the second floor, and bracing ourselves inside our coats, we made our way to our assigned room. The doorknob was frozen solid as we jammed the key into the keyhole. We struggled with the lock, while the icy air burned our lungs. Once inside we locked the door against the chill and did not venture out again until morning.

Back on the highway, as we ascended into the Canadian Rockies, we felt like we were entering no-man's land. The day's destination was Muncho Lake, 390 miles into the frozen wilderness. Signs of life were few and far between and the snow covered road merged with the rest of the landscape. The quiet isolation was peaceful, but as the day wore on and the temperature dropped dangerously low, we longed to get to the safety of our destined accommodation.

Muncho Lake Lodge! THIS is where we are spending the night? My heart sank as I inspected the lodge more closely with its low, snow-covered tin roof and partially rotted log walls. This is not a place I would stay, were there a choice; however, we needed to get inside as it was getting late, and colder by the minute. At least it would be warm. Very rustic, a worrisome smell of Raid Insect Spray lingered in our room. I wondered what the proprietors were trying to kill. After a decent hot meal in the café, Mark, exhausted from the drive, fell into a sound sleep. I, being very uncomfortable, lay awake thinking about what we were doing. For the first time I questioned our decision to embark on this journey. Had we made a mistake? Here we were, two Californians, deep in the wilds of Canada in the dead of winter about to cross into the Yukon Territory, and then on to Alaska. I missed my mommy.

The clear blue skies gave way to clouds, wind, and blowing snow as we departed from Muncho Lake. Soon we were once again the only two people in this colorless world. Driving became more stressful as the visibility worsened, and I noticed Mark looked stressed and exhausted. "Do you want me to drive for a while?" I asked, realizing there was no place to stop and rest. I had never driven in this kind of weather, but felt I could handle it. It was not like I was going to run into someone; we had the entire highway to ourselves. We pulled over, got out, stretched our legs, and I took over.

After adjusting to the feel of the snow and ice we rolled along uneventfully for a while. We gained elevation and the snow depth grew much deeper, causing the road to be less defined. As I hunched over the steering wheel, squinting into the glare, unexpectedly the truck started pulling strongly to the right. I didn't know what to do, or where the boundaries of the road were, and suddenly we were plowing through snow up to the windows as the truck bounced to a stop! We looked up as the snow settled like puffs of powder on the windshield - and knew we were in big trouble.

"You've really gotten us in a fix now!" Mark exclaimed. "I guess we better start digging ourselves out before we freeze to death." Luckily we had tools in the back.

I felt terrible as we surveyed our situation, and we knew we had no choice but to clear a path back on to the road… if we could find the road. I glanced in the direction we had come and seeing nothing but white, knew I had to start moving snow.

Thankfully we were not as alone as we had feared. The sound of a motor off in the distance brought us both to what we thought was the roadside. Through the obscurity of the darkening snow-filled daylight we could see them - headlights, growing brighter - and then as if by magic, a big, heaven-sent truck, with a winch attached to its bumper, materialized in all its glory! There is a God, and he came through for us that day.

"You folks need some help?" the driver asked as he surveyed our predicament. Mark and our rescuer attached the winch to our truck, and he effortlessly pulled us back onto the road.

Soon, with Mark back behind the wheel, and me in the doghouse, we proceeded towards the last frontier. So ended my experience of driving the infamous Alaska/Canada Highway. In my defense I will mention that we almost slid off the road and over a cliff while Mark manned the wheel. Our next stop was Whitehorse, Yukon Territory, and then on to Tok, Alaska, where we turned south and headed to Anchorage. Mike and Connie anxiously waited, and when we showed up at their place, pretty close to our estimated arrival time, we shared a joyous reunion.

Me, somewhere on the Alaska/Canada Highway

Chapter 4

THE LAST FRONTIER

We arrived in Anchorage in March of 1976 in the midst of the Alaska Pipeline Boom. The massive construction project was to bring oil from the North Slope of Alaska at Prudhoe Bay, spanning 800 miles, ending at the town of Valdez, situated on Prince William Sound. The oil is then pumped into storage tanks before being pumped onto oil tankers headed for the lower 48 states. Anchorage was bursting at the seams with cheechakos, the term old timers, known as sourdoughs, used for the hordes of newcomers. Luckily, Mike and Connie had a spare room all set up for us, knowing that we might be with them for a while. With the influx of oil industry workers and young professionals looking to take advantage of the opportunities this booming economy offered, no vacant housing units to buy or rent existed. They could not be built fast enough. We didn't mind sharing the apartment; none of us had much in the way of belongings, and we were delighted to be experiencing this exciting new adventure with our ski buddies.

FIRST DAY OF WORK

Our first order of business was to find jobs. Mark contacted the Carpenters' Union, and even though an abundance of work existed, the union was very discriminatory to newcomers, and he realized he would have to earn his way to membership. He immediately began to explore other avenues. I decided to go to an employment agency and see what options might be available to me before I went to Mike's father for a job with Standard Oil. The agency tested my typing and other secretarial skills and proceeded to book interviews for me. After a while the agent gave me a list of eleven companies I had appointments with the very next day. Eleven interviews in one day! I planned to be busy with my city map that evening.

Most of the meetings were not really interviews, but job offers. After introductions and pleasantries, the first question was "When can you start?" I was taken aback by this unexpected revelation, but soon realized that I was in the driver's seat. Instead of hoping for a job, I wondered which job I should choose. One of my options was joining the front desk staff in a busy medical clinic. The energy in the office drew me, people coming and going, phones constantly ringing, and a friendly, competent group of people who made it all function smoothly. I had gotten along well with the office manager, who actually interviewed me, and decided this was where I wanted to work. I was to start Monday morning.

Our first experience with an Alaskan snowstorm began Sunday evening, the day before I was to start my new job. Connie had arranged for Mike to drive her to work so I could borrow her car. My experience of driving in winter weather was limited to getting us stuck in a snowdrift on the Alaska/Canada Highway. I was not too worried as Connie told me she drove all over town in all kinds of conditions in her little Toyota, equipped with snow tires, with no problems. I had marked my route on the city map and planned to leave early in case the traffic was bad.

Monday morning three feet of new snow blanketed the neighborhood, which had not been plowed, and it was time to go! Connie instructed me to hit the gas pedal as I came down the driveway to build enough momentum to get me to the main road. "Stay in the tracks that we leave and you will be fine," she said. Now I was nervous. *I cannot get stuck,* I thought, *I will just have to plow through it.* With my gloved hands gripping the frozen steering wheel and the engine revved, I floored it, and blasted down the driveway and out onto the deep, new snow.

With snow flying all around I kept my speed up with my eyes trained on the crossroad ahead, a more traveled road where I hoped the snow would be packed down. Once there, I eased into a right turn and to my relief, the road was manageable. From there I was to turn left on Northern Lights Blvd, a major thoroughfare on which the medical clinic was located. *Whew, I think I can do this,* I thought. At the intersection I turned onto Northern Lights Blvd. wondering why there was no traffic. The snow was still on the road and had not been packed much by other drivers. *What is that up ahead?* It looked like a road block. As I approached the large "ROAD CLOSED" sign, I knew I was in trouble. There was no one at the road block and no way to turn around, so I turned down a side street leading who knew where? *I will just have to stop and get new directions,* I told myself. I drove around a residential area looking for any signs of life, getting further and further off course while the clock ticked closer to 9 a.m. Just as I began to panic, I spotted a convenience store up ahead. I pulled into the parking lot and found a place to park among the mountains of snow that had been plowed aside. *I hope I don't get stuck here,* I told myself as my car slid to a stop. I got out and called the office manager at the clinic and explained my predicament. Aware of the road closure, she gave me directions from where I was and told me to take my time driving in the snow.

I was mortified to be showing up on the first day at Medical Park twenty minutes late. But due to the storm, other employees were late and very few patients had shown up for their appointments. I was reassured and welcomed into the office by the staff and settled into what would be my introduction to life in Anchorage, Alaska.

Medical Park was a very busy business. I soon learned that everyone in Anchorage, and many people from the outlying areas came there for all of their medical needs - not only scheduled appointments, but minor, and some major emergencies showed up at our door. There was only one hospital in Anchorage, and with the population increasing by the minute, the emergency room there was usually overcrowded. During business hours, everyone came to Medical Park to avoid long waits at the emergency room. After working there for a year, I think I had met everyone in town at least once. I really enjoyed interacting face to face with such a compelling mix of sourdoughs and cheechakos. The sourdoughs (mostly men) with their beards, worn jeans and flannel shirts, together with the cheechakos (also mostly men) in business suits and overcoats. There were also women, but during the construction of the Alaska Pipeline, it was estimated that men outnumbered women in the state by ten to one. I don't know how accurate this estimation was, but I do know there were a lot of men. It was unheard of for a woman to open a door for herself or scrape the ice off of her windshield. When a female needed something done, there was always a man or three around to do it for her. Ah, how I miss that aspect of living in Alaska.

While I spent my days at the medical clinic, Mark found non-union work to fill his time until he was accepted into the union. Mike and Connie's family and friends soon became our Alaskan family and friends. We learned to ice skate, went skiing as the daylight lengthened, and enjoyed cozy dinners by the fire, all the while waiting for an apartment of our own to become available. One of Mike's coworkers and his wife had purchased a condominium that neared completion. When we heard this news we asked if we could inherit their apartment when they moved. The demand was so high for housing units that most places had a waiting list, but the couple agreed to meet with their manager and see if we could have the apartment once their condominium was finished.

One month after arriving in Anchorage we moved into our newly vacated, two bedrooms, one bath, second-floor apartment. The small complex was fairly new and centrally located. With the help of a coworker and a neighborhood-moving sale, we secured all the necessary furnishings and settled in.

Spring is not the most pleasant season in the northland. The snow and ice melt, creating slush, and then refreeze, creating slick and slippery road conditions. As the snow melts for good, the emerging earth is brown and lifeless. Being from California, we had never experienced the changing of the seasons and found the transformation interesting and tolerable. During this time Mark received the news that he was at last a card-carrying member of the Carpenters' Local and joined the crews of tradesmen who changed the town of Anchorage into the city it was to become.

Me in front of Portage Glacier

As spring progressed, the days began to grow long and almost overnight grass greened, trees became full, and flowers colored the hillsides. One bright and sunny day in late May, I returned to the clinic after lunch, prepared for a busy afternoon of checking in patients and answering phones and scheduling appointments. It seemed really quiet in the usually packed waiting room and I checked the clock to see if it was earlier than I thought. It wasn't, and most of our 2:00 p.m. patients had not shown up. I went to ask what was going on only to discover none of the four doctors were in their offices either. One of the nurses came in the back door and I asked her where everyone was. "They are all at the park." She answered nonchalantly.

"At the park?" I questioned. "What are they doing there? It's 2:10 p.m."

"The sun is out!" she exclaimed. "Everyone is outside."

Californians take sunny days for granted. I had no idea that warm, clear days were so rare in Anchorage. So rare (especially the first warm day after the long winter), that they were treated like state holidays. Not returning to work after lunch was kind of expected. Eventually the staff returned and most of the patients showed up, but everyone remained in such a good mood you would have thought it was Christmas. And so began the spectacular summer of 1976.

The sun shone almost every day (and night) that summer. In June, the sun never really sets completely in and around Anchorage. There are a few hours of twilight between 12:30 a.m. and 2:30 a.m., but no real darkness. With so much sunlight the plants grow profusely, and Alaska is awash in the lush colors of summer. We could not get enough of the great outdoors. As soon as we got off work on Friday afternoon, we packed the truck with our camping, fishing, and hiking gear. Together with Mike and Connie, and sometimes other friends, we would head south to the Kenai Peninsula, or north to whichever river the salmon were running in. Regardless of the hour we arrived and got our campsite set up, the guys would head out to fish, sometimes until the wee hours of the morning.

As the summer progressed we fell in love with Alaska; the long hours of sunlight, the majestic mountains covered with wildflowers and wildlife, the rivers teeming with fish that we grilled on our campfire within hours of being caught, all conspired to capture our hearts. Our plan to experience the northland for a year or two and return to California was soon forgotten. Mike's mom warned us that we were experiencing an exceptionally warm, clear summer, and that these dry summers only come around about every seven years. However, arriving in the state just in time to see Alaska at the height of its magnificence left us all with a lasting impression that would keep us there for years to come.

Mark on a typical day off

THE WILDLIFE

One evening early in that stunning summer, Mark, Mike, Connie and I were heading home from a dinner party with friends, which went quite late. We marveled that it was still light at that late hour, as we turned a corner to be silenced by a crystal clear view of

Mount McKinley, glowing pink in the midnight sun. We pulled over, got out of the car, and quietly basked in the unique beauty that is Alaska. The sky was softly blue with wispy white clouds while a surreal aura settled itself around us. No one spoke as we stood silently absorbing the splendor before us.

Mount McKinley in the midnight sun.

Our camping trips were filled with unexpected adventure. The abundance of wildlife made for some fun, and sometimes frightening, encounters. Moose were everywhere. We saw them in the meadows munching grasses, standing in shallow rivers and lakes, sometimes with a newborn calf. We saw them in our yards, especially in the winter, meandering around like they owned the place. The bear encounters proved a little more alarming, even though it was usually black bears raiding our campsites, looking for the fish we had just caught. Typically, black bears do not threaten humans, but they are still bears and we kept our distance.

One Sunday afternoon, Mark was grilling some of our fresh caught salmon for a late lunch before heading back to town. Mike, Connie and I were packing the vehicles when Connie, always on bear patrol, spotted a bear heading right for our camp. "Get in the truck!" she shouted. Mike and I looked up at the same time and dove into the nearest vehicle. Apparently, Mark had not heard

Connie's warning, because he continued grilling our fish as if nothing was amiss. He finally looked up, wondering where everyone had gone, just as the bear entered the campsite behind him.

"Holy crap!" he shouted when he finally spotted the bear. He dropped the fish rack into the fire and bolted for the truck. Once inside he lambasted me for leaving him out there with the bear, but I thought he had heard Connie's warning - and besides, we were all in survival mode. We watched the bear mosey on through our camp and on down to the river without a glance at us, or our fish. He must have already eaten.

The Alaskan Brown Bear, or grizzly bear, is another story, and an encounter with one of them could be deadly. We learned that first summer to always carry a powerful firearm, while exploring the wilds. Mark and Mike had a close encounter with a very large brown bear one evening along the river. The bear watched them defensively from his feeding spot where he snatched salmon from the river, while they slowly slinked from his vision, and then ran like lightning back to camp.

More frightening than the Alaskan Brown Bear are the large and ever present Alaskan mosquitoes. These buggers are relentlessly annoying, and unstoppable. No matter how much repellant you apply, they will find a way to get you: through your clothes, hair, or any exposed skin not covered with Cutter's Insect Repellant. The smell of Cutter's, the only repellent that seemed to work against them, signaled the first sign that summer had arrived in Anchorage.

Chapter 5

LIFE IS OUR OYSTER

By September of our first year in Alaska, we were hooked. Hooked on being outdoors, hiking, camping and fishing, during the long days of that spectacular summer. We were there to stay, at least for a while. The next lesson we learned about Alaska was that summer is very short. One day it is sunny and warm, and the next there is termination dust (snow) on the local mountaintops. The days grew short and the temperature dropped. Every day was a new experience for us thin-blooded Californians. We learned from friends about studded snow tires and plugging in engine heaters on cars left outside overnight. I learned the hard way about wearing proper shoes and carrying my heels to work. I also learned the hard way to avoid the infamous Tudor Road, a main thoroughfare running from the west side of town to the east. As I mentioned, Anchorage was a boomtown at this time and the narrow two-lane Tudor Road was in the process of being widened when winter arrived, before the road could be paved. Drivers were forced to drive on the gravel base, which was freezing and thawing repeatedly. Giant, and I mean giant, pot holes began to form, and Tudor Road became a challenge to be reckoned with. Thinking I was an Alaskan now, and should be able to navigate myself around town in all conditions, I observed other drivers meeting the challenge, and together with my Toyota Corolla, attempted to conquer Tudor Road. The mounds of earth were four or five feet high, and the valleys between them where slick with ice and mud, a virtual obstacle course. After I arrived safely at my destination, I knew why people sported bumper stickers that read: "I Drove Tudor Road and Survived." It was not a joke. That road could have eaten you alive.

INVESTING

During that first full northland winter, we settled into our new jobs. I enjoyed working with the public and meeting many locals who frequented our clinic. Mark learned what it was like to build commercial buildings in freezing temperatures and little-to-no daylight. We both made good money, and our savings account began to grow.

After work we went ice-skating, joined friends on their snow machines (snow mobiles), or stayed inside to watch a favorite TV show. As we moved toward spring, and more daylight hours, we would ski at Alyeska, our local ski resort. The skiing posed more of a challenge with the extreme weather and limited daylight, but we got out there as often as conditions allowed.

Once again we were in awe, as the landscape was now a crystalline, sparkling wonderland; the hoar frost coated trees, the frozen waterfalls layered with icy blue colors, and the local mountains greeting us each day in snowy white majesty. Living amidst nature's grandeur was becoming normal to us, and we woke up each morning excited to venture out.

During this time Mike and Connie had purchased their first home, and we began to think about a house for ourselves. Mark's mother had invested in real estate after his father's death, and we hoped to do the same as our finances allowed. With no intention of returning to the Bay Area any time soon, we decided to sell our condominium back home and use the money to buy a house in Anchorage. Surprisingly, we learned that our condo in California had increased in value, and it sold quickly. With our first real estate profit tucked safely away, we began to think about our financial future.

Connie called me at work one morning, telling me about a cute little house in her neighborhood that had just gone up for sale. The housing shortage had eased somewhat with all the new construction, but you still had to act fast, as properties did not remain on the market for long. I called immediately and made an appointment to see the house that evening.

We closed the deal on the Blackberry Road house a few weeks later for the asking price of $83,000. After a coat of paint, new carpet, and a few miscellaneous repairs, we moved in. Our new home was adorable, with three bedrooms, a bath-and-a-half, a workable kitchen with a window overlooking our large backyard. The house, however, lacked a fireplace, so Mark went to work building a beautiful stone fireplace and soon we were snug as two bugs in our little house with the snow piled high outside and the glow of firelight warming us inside. With the rest of the money from the sale of our condo, and some of our quickly growing savings accounts, we bought our first investment property, a duplex that we rented, and maintained ourselves.

Me in front of the Blackberry house

~

Anchorage had the feel of a town when we arrived, but it was growing into a city before our eyes. On weekends when we were not skiing or camping, we would drive around and look at all the new building projects and home developments, always mindful of investment opportunities. One early spring Sunday, Mike, Connie, Mark, and I loaded into the cab of Mark's four-wheel-drive pickup, with the intent of viewing a property for sale that sounded promising. The house was up Huffman Road, one of three roads that went up the mountainside, overlooking Anchorage. This was a desirable and pricey part of town, due to the alpine setting, daytime views of the inlet, and, at night, the city lights below. Not as desirable were the steep, hazardous roads. The hillside residents all had four-wheel-drive vehicles, as did we, and we did not give road conditions a second thought that clear morning. Our directions took us to a long, straight, steep climbing road. Mark made sure the four-wheel-drive was engaged, and we headed up. Clear roads and bright skies greeted us that day; however, the temperature remained well below freezing. Up, up, up we went, with a sheer drop off to our right. Suddenly we felt the tires slip slightly. "Is that black ice on the road?" Mike asked.

"I think it is," replied Mark, as we all strained to look over the dashboard. "There is no room to turn around; should I back down, or keep going?" Before anyone could voice an opinion, the wheels began to spin on the ice and the truck started sliding backwards. Mark had absolutely no control of the steering or brakes. Without realizing it, we had been on ice the whole time, and when we reached a steeper section of the hill, we lost traction, and were at the mercy of the ice. No one said anything, but we all believed we were about to die, as we looked behind us at the long, steep road - and the cliff so very close. Slowly we slid, as we held our breaths and subconsciously leaned towards the mountainside. By the grace of God, the truck slid as straight as an arrow all the way back down. When we reached safety, we all exhaled and sat in silence until we stopped shaking. At this point we all agreed that even though we hadn't seen it, the property at the top of the hill was probably not one that we would be investing in. We turned around and went back home.

~

My one complaint about my job at the medical clinic was that sick or injured people turned up frequently just before closing, needing care. The office policy was to stay until everyone who needed treatment was taken care of. Consequently, I got home very late many days, and I began to look for another job. My first stop was at Wien Air Alaska, an Anchorage-based airline flying mostly within the state. The receptionist told me they were interviewing for flight attendants, handed me an application, and scheduled me for an interview a few days later. When I arrived for my interview, I immediately recognized the chief flight attendant as one of our regular patients at the clinic. She was expecting me, as I had listed my current employment at Medical Park on the application. She already knew how I interacted with the public - luckily for me we had had pleasant interactions - and liked that I was working in a medical environment, even though my job was answering phones and greeting patients. The interview went well and the very next day she called, letting me know I would be starting my training in a couple of weeks, which gave me just enough time to give notice at Medical Park. That night as I lay in bed, I wondered what it would be like to be a flight attendant for Wien Air Alaska. I was excited, however, a little bit scared.

AURORA BOREALIS

Even though March signals the end of winter in many parts of the world, Anchorage did not welcome spring so readily. By now we had more normal daylight, clear skies, as happens more in winter, and a temperature well below zero, especially at night. Mark has never been a heavy sleeper, and for some reason several nights in a row he found himself up wandering around the house wide awake. He mentioned to a co-worker that he had not been able to sleep lately. The co-worker explained that the northern lights activity might be the cause. "What does that have to do with me not sleeping?" Mark asked.

"The northern lights (aurora borealis) are a result of certain atmospheric conditions that disturb some peoples' sleep, the same way a full moon can affect people. In fact, we have a northern lights hot line. The people that are awakened by the lights have lists of people who want to be called, so they can get up and see them too."

"I have been up all week, but I have not looked outside," Mark answered. "If I wake up again tonight, I will check the sky".

The next night, crystal clear and very cold, sure enough, Mark woke and decided to step outside to see what he could see. Neither of us had witnessed the aurora and really did not know what to look for, or expect. Mark was astounded as he stepped out into another of nature's wonders. The sky literally danced, putting on a show of colors and movement. He rushed in to wake me. "You've got to get up and see this!" Mark exclaimed. "Hurry before they go away." He rushed back outside while I grabbed my robe and slippers.

As soon as I stepped out the door, the spectacle overhead mesmerized me. We slowly made our way to the center of the street, following the movement of the lights as they flitted about the black sky, one second greens and yellows, the next purples and blues. Light and color moved in waves and flashes, and we just watched, stunned by this spectacular show. I don't know how long we stood there in our robes and slippers, but eventually the cold brought us back to our senses. We seriously needed to get inside, but would the show be over when we came back out in warmer clothes? Eventually, the colors began to fade, and the lights became a cloud-like shadow. We assumed the best was over and scrambled back indoors. Too excited to sleep, we jumped back in bed, wrapped up in our blankets, and shared our thoughts and questions about this magical performance nature had just put on for us. From then on, if Mark couldn't sleep, we were up, out of bed, checking the sky.

A moose in our front yard

WIEN AIR ALASKA

Am I in the right place? I wondered as I parked in front of one of the gigantic airplane hangars at Anchorage International Airport on that clear April morning of 1977. My first day of training, I hadn't expected to be in a hangar. After double-checking the address, I found a door and tentatively went inside. Mechanics in overalls climbed in and out of planes, and I felt small and insignificant in such a cavernous space. One of the mechanics spotted me and came over to offer assistance.

"You must be here for the new flight attendant class," he stated with a friendly grin. I told him I was, feeling relieved as he directed me up a long flight of less than sturdy stairs that led to a wooden walk-way high up along the side of the hangar wall. I felt so out of place, at the same time excited, to be entering into this new world. Once inside what would serve as our classroom, I recognized Marion, the chief flight attendant, who was there to greet me.

Twenty-four new hires attended the six-week training class, and we soon came to friendly terms with each other.

There was a lot more to learn than I had anticipated. Emergency procedures and first-aid took up most of our training hours. Learning our way around the aircrafts - jumping and sliding down the evacuations slides, water ditching practice in a swimming pool, and all the FAA regulations that had to be strictly followed - made for a vigorous training course. A fellow flight attendant trainee who had previously worked for two other airlines commented that the Wien flight attendant's training was far more extensive than the other airlines she had worked for. Keep in mind where we were flying - remote villages only accessible by air, pipeline construction camps as far north as Prudhoe Bay, and many times landing Boeing 737s on short gravel airstrips.

Near the end of the course, time came for our anticipated training flights. We would accompany crews as trainees for two flights before our final written tests and graduation. When Marion announced I would be training on flight 19, everyone in the room gasped and shook their heads, looking at me with anxious eyes. "What is the issue with flight 19?" I asked. "Why the concern?"

I was quickly brought up to speed on the infamous flight 19, which carried pipeline workers back and forth from Anchorage to Prudhoe Bay, with a stop in Fairbanks. The workers headed to weeks of working twelve hours a day, seven days a week in subzero temperature darkness. Flight 19 was their last chance to have a few drinks, see anything resembling a female, and enjoy a last ninety minutes of freedom. The return flight would be carrying the workers out that these workers were replacing. This was their first opportunity to re-enter society, and for a group of young men who had been in this frozen wasteland for a couple of weeks, they entered it with pent-up energy, ordering drinks as we greeted them at the door.

Most of flight 19 passengers were regulars who knew the flight attendants that worked this flight, and the flight attendants knew them and knew what they were in store for. Flight 19 was known and accepted as a flying party. I, however, had no idea.

To make my first training flight as bad as it possibly could be, I was given a partial uniform, which marked me as a trainee. Every passenger on the flight decided it would be great fun to break me in before we returned to Anchorage. I was teased, made fun of, and harassed mercilessly until I was literally in tears. I had not considered I would be dealing with unruly out-of-control passengers. I told the other flight attendants that this was not for me, and I was quitting as soon as we got back to town. Thankfully they both worked Flight 19 regularly, and went on to scold the passengers, who they knew to be good guys, and told them I was sufficiently initiated as a crew-member of Flight 19.

I survived that first training flight and went on to work Flight 19 many, many times over the eight years I was with Wien. I never had a problem after that and learned that the pipeline workers were just young, fun-loving guys who meant no harm, as long as we got the drinks out fast enough.

~

Every day was an adventure working for this historic airline. Noel Wien made the first flight from Anchorage to Fairbanks in 1924. Soon after, he started the first passenger airline in Alaska, and one of the first airlines in the United States. He began with open cockpit biplanes carrying one passenger - dressed in really warm clothes, I hope! - operating under the name of Northern Air Transport. The company incorporated in 1929 and became Wien Alaska Airlines in 1936. Wien's aircraft were always required to operate in extraordinary conditions, and the airline later purchased Boeing 737s specifically modified to land on gravel runways. These unique 737s also had cargo doors built into the side of the fuselage to allow for cargo containers to be loaded into the cabin in place of removable passenger seats. During the long cold winter, many routes had few passengers, and Wien transported needed supplies to remote villages. I still worked for Wien when they ceased operation in 1985 as the second oldest airline in the United States.

Wien flight attendants boarding an infant in an incubator.
Date unknown.
Photo from the Internet.

Wien transported all types of cargo, even a herd of reindeer.
Date unknown. Photo from the Internet

I never worried about safety. Mostly Alaskans, the pilots working for Wien flew their own private airplanes, and were highly skilled at navigating in extreme conditions. They would also take liberties that I can't imagine a pilot for any other airline taking. Early in my career with Wien, I was in the cockpit delivering coffee and noticed the active volcano, Mount Redoubt, spewing steam up ahead. The pilot asked if I had seen it up close, and when I responded in the negative, he banked the aircraft and proceeded to circle the rim of the volcano, offering me a birds-eye view of the smoldering crater. I was a little surprised that we could veer off course spontaneously, but along with the tourists, loved every minute of it. On another unusually clear summer day, the pilot announced that since Mount McKinley was gloriously free of its usual clouds and fog, we would be taking a scenic detour and proceeded to circle the peaks and glide through the valleys of this majestic mountain. Passengers as well as crew were in awe of this once in a lifetime experience. During the cold, dark winter, many of our flights were "cargo" flights. A few seats would be left for passengers, but sometimes there were none. On those occasions we were allowed to ride in the cockpit with the pilots, and on nights when the northern lights were active, there was no better way to watch them. Going to work for me was never just another day at the office.

Me with a Wien pilot. Early 1980's

A fellow flight attendant and I with a gate agent. Kotzebo, Alaska

We were the only lifeline to civilization for the native people, the pipeline workers, and the hunters and fisherman out in the wilds. There was little to no medical care outside of Fairbanks and Anchorage, and injured or sick patients, and pregnant women in labor, were loaded onto our flights as we headed back towards the hospital in Anchorage. The local nurse or medical assistant would brief us - the flight attendants - on the patients' status, and then left us to manage their care on our own. We monitored their IVs, which hung from the coat racks (no bins in those days) above them. We also timed labor pains, and held the hands of scared, injured construction workers, all the while praying that nothing happened before we got to town. In this environment, it was necessary for us to have more extensive first aide/medical training than the crew-members of other airlines, and emergencies did happen. Somewhere there is a woman named McKinley, who was born on a Wien flight, as the plane flew by the mountain of the same name. I personally never had to deliver a baby, but some of my fellow flight attendants did.

Flying past Mount McKinley.

THE FIREWEED GLASSES

I don't know if life could have been any better for us at this time. Our second summer in Alaska was filled with exploration and discoveries. I flew out to all of the remote locations of the last frontier, and Mark labored long hours as construction tried to keep up with the population growth. He worked on commercial buildings in town and was in his element. The money was flowing, and we continued to grow our savings. We still escaped to the great outdoors whenever we could, eating our fresh catch of salmon, trout, or grayling, and smoking what we couldn't eat. Along with the smell of Cutter's insect spray, the smell of fish smoking permeated the air all summer. As Mike's mother had warned, that next summer arrived drizzly and damp. We quickly adapted and did not let a little drizzle keep us indoors.

Mark's fishing buddy, Jim, from back home, now divorced, joined us that summer to experience the last frontier. On Friday afternoons, the three of us would load the truck with our camping gear and drive south along Turnagain Arm, a branch of Cook Inlet, to the Kenai Peninsula. Beautiful mountains, ablaze with fireweed, a tall, lance shaped, pinkish, purple showy flower, surround the inlet. One Friday afternoon about midsummer, the Fireweed was strikingly vivid, and I exclaimed at its beauty each time we turned a corner, revealing a new view. Mark and Jim did not comment and I asked if they didn't find the mountainsides just spectacular. They shrugged and said they were nice like they always were, leaving me baffled, because the colors were extraordinary. After a stop, Jim picked up my sunglasses off the dashboard by mistake and put them on. "Oh my gosh! Look at that fireweed!" he marveled as we got back on the road. "It really is gorgeous!" When I realized he had on my sunglasses, we discovered the lenses had a purple tint to them that intensified the color of the Fireweed dramatically. We all wanted to wear the "Fireweed glasses" from then on. We took turns wearing them and even purchased more purple-tinted sunglasses, but never found another pair that lit up our view like the "Fireweed glasses".

LAKE ILLIAMNA

Working for an airline has the benefit of all benefits, airline passes!!! The passes are not limited to the airline you work for, but for all airlines. For a small processing fee – at the time it was $30.00 – we could go anywhere in the world! We took advantage of this most excellent benefit during the long northern winters. During the summer we used our passes to get to some of the world's best fishing spots in our new home state. Across the inlet from Anchorage, on the far side of the Alaska Mountain range, was the renowned fishing mecca of Lake Illiamna.

By our second summer we felt like sourdoughs (seasoned Alaskans), compared with the stream of newcomers still flowing into the state. Mark, being quite an accomplished fisherman, decided it was time we broadened our horizons, using our passes to get deeper into the wilderness. Wien had recently started flying a specially modified Boeing 737 into the fishing village of Lake Illiamna to accommodate the elite sportsmen of the world. To land a jet at this undeveloped airport, the pilots had to initiate a heart-stopping dive after crossing the peaks of the Alaska Range, to reach the beginning of the short, gravel airstrip, designed for small air taxies and private planes. As soon as the plane touched down on the gravel, the brakes were immediately and forcefully applied to stop the plane within the limits of this relatively minuscule airstrip. Most of the Illiamna passengers were wealthy (it was expensive getting to, and staying in these fishing camps), and experienced travelers, used to luxury and pampering. I would cringe when the women boarded in Anchorage in their high heels and the men in their brand spanking new fishing vests with unused flies and lures attached, because I knew they were ill-prepared. When we hit the runway, gravel and rocks flew and shrieks and screams came from the unsuspecting passengers, mostly from the Lower 48, who thought we were crash landing. We quickly informed them that this was a perfectly normal landing - for Wien Air Alaska anyway - and that their fishing guides would soon meet them. Some of them were a little shaken by the landing, and then, when they saw they were to deplane on to the muddy, rocky, dirty runway, they were aghast!

Some deplaned looking anxious, while others had their noses out of joint. Welcome to Alaska! After comments and complaints from passengers, we began preparing them in advance, explaining the necessity for the abrupt and frightening landing. With advance notice they began to enjoy the thrill of their first Alaskan experience.

I did enjoy working that particular flight and learning where the passengers were from and their expectations, and then to see them again on their return a week or so later to hear their impressions. Many times it turned out that their expectations had been totally wrong; however, what they did experience turned out to be unforgettably fantastic. I remember one gentleman in particular because he boarded in Anchorage with his new fishing gear and outfit, looking every bit the inexperienced fisherman. On his return I noticed the gear still looked unused and new. I asked how his trip was and he responded, "Even though I didn't catch any fish, I had the time of my life." I pondered how a person could spend a week at Lake Illiamna in the middle of summer, with a guide, and not catch fish. I was disappointed for him, but I was happy that he didn't seem to care, and was on a natural high just from being there.

~

"The Newhalen River is just a mile from the runway at Illiamna airport, so we can fly over with our backpacks, head down to the river and find a spot to set up camp." Mark's plan seemed simple enough. We had a few days off and thought we would use some passes and fly over to Lake Illiamna. Thinking we knew how to survive in the Alaskan wilderness by now, we purchased new sturdy backpacks to support all of the necessary gear - which was a lot - and began packing for three nights of camping.

We knew the weather could be wet and/or cold, we could get stuck if the flights couldn't get in, and might be out there longer than anticipated, and that we might not catch enough fish to eat, so the packs got heavier and heavier. Mark's ended up weighing seventy pounds with all his fishing gear, including waders, and mine wasn't much lighter with all the cooking supplies. We figured we only had about a mile to walk, so no problem.

When we got to Lake Illiamna, we discovered clear weather, mild temperatures, and the salmon running in the Newhalen. The Wien gate agents told us the trout fishing had been good also. They directed us to the trail leading to the river, and with their assistance strapped our monstrous packs on our backs and we headed out. The scenery was spectacular. By midsummer the landscape is as green as green can be, dotted with patches of wild berries, and framed by white peaks in every direction. We walked off the end of the runway in what we thought was the right direction. After a while we began to wonder if we were on the right trail. We could hear the roar of the rapids from the mighty Newhalen, but seemed to be walking away from it. It was time to change course.

To our left there was a large green field and the sound of the river. In our innocence, we decided to cut across the field and save ourselves the effort of taking what seemed to be the long way around. Once well into the field we realized there was a reason the trail went around it. With each step we sunk up to our knees in what we soon learned was tundra. Balancing our packs and pulling our legs up and out became a monumental effort. Stopping to catch our breath, sinking deeper and deeper, we knew we had made a mistake. We had heard about and seen tundra from a distance, but did not know the structure of it. The subsoil remains permanently frozen, hindering tree growth but supporting moss, lichen and certain berries. During the warm months this top layer thaws and becomes a soggy, spongy blanket of growth. Looking ahead we still had a long way to go, and had come too far to go back. We were stuck.

"Let's take off our packs, leave them here and go on ahead to see how far it is to the river, find a campsite, and then come back and get the packs," Mark reasoned. "We can bring them out one at a time, sharing the weight, or take items out separately if that is what it takes to get everything to camp." It sounded like a good plan to me, anything to get us out of the quicksand-like tundra.

Without the packs, though still a struggle, we managed to make it to the river where we found a sheltered spot suitable to pitch our tent. Leaving the items we had brought with us, we headed back to the bog to retrieve our packs and the rest of our gear. Looking out over the expanse of the field, we saw no sign of our brightly colored backpacks. We left them laying in plain sight, clearly visible from all directions. *Where did they go? Were we in the right place?* We thought that we were, but for some reason we could not see the packs.

We had no choice but to trudge back into the field and begin a search. The huge field bore no landmarks of any kind. It was getting late and we were tired, but we needed our gear. We did not have to worry about losing daylight, but the sun was getting weaker, and it was clouding up and beginning to drizzle. Where were those backpacks?

Up and down the field we searched. Each step was an effort as the tundra grabbed at our legs as if it would pull us under. After what seemed an eternity, Mark spotted the orange of my pack deep down and totally submerged in the mossy, spongy, growth. The heavy packs had been swallowed up and were totally hidden from sight. It is amazing that we found them and were able to recover them. With great effort we got all of our equipment to what would be our home for the next few days. Lesson learned: stay on the trail when backpacking in Alaska!

Mark fished all day while I explored the area, finding wild berries, watching the birds soaring overhead, and reading my ever present novel - always on alert for the bears that fished the river too. The mist and drizzle continued, adding to the mystique of this rugged and wild sportsman's paradise. In the evening we cooked our fresh salmon on our campfire, and Mark filleted and packed the rest of the day's catch in a plastic bag, tied it to a large rock, and let it dangle in the icy river to keep it fresh. In the morning he went down to check on his fish, and to his dismay all that remained was the knot of the bag still tied to the rock. Scraps of the bag, along with pieces of fish bones, were scattered along the rocky shore. The local bears were smarter than we were, finding a meal all filleted and packaged up for them. Mark was not happy, as if we didn't have plenty of salmon, and headed back out to fish.

Flying out to Lake Illiamna became a summer tradition. Mark started taking his friend Paul, and I stayed home, allowing them a guy's weekend. They always came home with great stories, usually bear stories, and of course a lot of fresh fish.

Mark's brother Dave, just before a big surprise.

THE ACCIDENT

When I first woke up I didn't know where I was. I had a few memories flitting around in my head: A vision/dream of my brother hovering in my hospital room, my nose being brutally yanked back into place, and a cast being applied to my leg. I noticed my mom sitting beside me and began to realize I must be seriously sick or injured, but where was my dad? As my surroundings came into focus, Mom noticed I was awake. She was very excited and called for the nurse. Taking my hand, she greeted me with a kiss to my forehead, while a tear escaped from her glistening eyes.

I was shocked to learn I had been semi-comatose for the better part of two weeks and had no memory of what had happened to me, or for that matter, no memory at all of the last few years of my life. *Alaska? What was I doing in Alaska?* Gradually Mark explained to me that I had left for work one morning for an early check-in, and had been in a head-on automobile accident. I had been driving my Toyota Corolla, which did not offer driver or passengers much protection. I smashed my knees on the dashboard, broke my steering wheel in half with my face, before whiplashing so hard I suffered a serious concussion and neck and back injuries, not to mention broken ribs and several cuts and bruises. I was a mess! Luckily, before the Neurosurgeon had to drill holes in my skull to relieve pressure, one of the medications he was using to reduce the swelling in my brain began to work.

As the days passed and the injuries slowly healed, I struggled to remember what had caused me to cross over into on-coming traffic. To this day I have no memory of the accident, or the events of the morning before the accident. It took years before I regained most of my memory, but I never regained any memory of the accident or the time leading up to it.

Mark and/or my mother stayed by my bedside all day long. They told me how close to death I had come and how terrified they had been. I told Mark that I had a memory of Jim, my deceased brother, being in the hospital room with me. I remembered seeing him from the shoulders up, serenely hovering near the ceiling and looking around the room, as if he were making sure I was being properly cared for. It was such a vivid picture, seeming more real than a dream. Mark then proceeded to tell me he had had a strange experience, too. A few days after the accident, before my mother arrived, the doctor had told him I might not survive the night, and in his anguish he went to the hospital chapel. Feeling alone and helpless, he began to pray and asked God not to take me from him. At the depths of his despair, he suddenly felt a comforting hand on his shoulder, and at the same time a wave of comfort moved through him, along with the knowledge that I was going to be okay. He couldn't explain why, but he then knew I would come through this ordeal, and he left the chapel feeling optimistic.

Had my brother's spirit been with us during this time of crisis? Was he there to offer comfort and strength? Or was I at death's door, and he had come to escort me to the other side? We both left the hospital feeling that we had been visited by Jim's spirit. The impression Jim left with us, if it was him, is that there is an afterlife, and that it is probably a beautiful thing.

My doctors sent me home to heal with a plan to return to the hospital in six weeks for surgery to repair my left knee, expecting my brain to be well enough by then to withstand the operation. Everything went as planned, and after a long leave of absence, I longed to get back to work. I was mentally fragile for a long time, with stubborn memory loss, forgetfulness, and the inability to focus. I never fully recovered from that serious concussion, and now struggle with Attention Deficit Disorder. However, I am lucky to have survived, and have learned how to cope with this challenging disorder.

FAMOUS PEOPLE

Soon I was back to work, greeting passengers from all over the world, serving drinks as fast as we could, and visiting remote native villages, pipeline construction camps, and some of the world's best fishing and hunting destinations. Later I wondered why I did not carry a camera with me to work each day. During my eight years working at Wien, I encountered many unique and famous people with whom I could have taken photos. However, when you live somewhat removed from the more civilized Lower 48, fame and fortune become less important. Alaskans are more impressed by nature's majesty, adventure, and freedom, and less impressed by a movie star.

Growing up in California I had been exposed to celebrities from a very young age. We spent many weekends at Lake Tahoe and encountered performers like Jack Benny, Tom Jones, and

Liberace, as they enjoyed their time off around the lake. When I was about ten-years-old, Dad took me to the 1964 groundbreaking ceremony of the Bay Area Rapid Transit system (BART), presided over by none other than President Lyndon Johnson. Dad maneuvered me right up to the president, who put his hand on my head to step around me. I looked up, up, and up, until I finally saw the face of this really tall man.

Movie stars and professional athletes venture to Alaska for fishing, hunting, and other types of adventures, including The Great Alaskan Bush Company, a local tradition featuring "exotic" dancers from around the world. During the pipeline construction years, the Bush Company became world renowned - at least among exotic dancers - for the huge amounts of money their customers were willing to part with. Workers coming back to town after weeks on the North Slope, with literally pockets full of money, couldn't get to the Bush Company fast enough. Some of them left most of that money in the G-strings of the dancers. Word spread through the exotic dancing world, and the best "equipped" performers made their way to the Bush Company. These dancers were famed as the best and best-looking the exotic dance world had to offer. The "men only," except for one night a week, club, was as frequented as Mt. McKinley (now Denali) National Park. On a night that ladies were allowed, a group of us took Mark's youngest brother, who was visiting from California to experience this renowned club. The males in our group bought Dave a table dance. This was before we knew he was gay. Anyway, we all got to experience The Great Alaskan Bush Company, which is still popular today.

My most noteworthy passengers include: Jack Lemmon and his son Chris, Robert Redford, Ted Nugent, the rocker known as the Detroit Mad Man, Maria Muldaur, sports greats whose names I don't remember, and exceptional people like Red Adair, the famous wildcatter, who later put out the Kuwait oil fires set by Saddam

Hussein, and many others. These people were exciting to meet, but they don't compare to my encounter with the Pope.

JOHN PAUL II

The new Polish Pope, John Paul II, had come to Anchorage. *What a great opportunity to see a pope*, I thought. Anchorage was a relatively small town and who would travel all the way up here to see the pope? He was to celebrate Mass downtown on the park strip at noon. I don't remember the exact date, sometime in the very early 1980s, and I was off work and headed downtown to join what I expected to be a manageable crowd to hear the pope say Mass. I don't know where all of the people came from, but I could not get near the park strip. Stuck in traffic for forty minutes, as a light rain began to fall, I decided I was not prepared for the weather or the crowd. A few years in Alaska ruins a person for dealing with large crowds and traffic jams. I turned off as soon as I was able, and went back home to watch the service on television.

While preparing to go to work the next day, I heard on the news that the pope was making his way to the airport for his departure from Alaska. I worried about the traffic congestion this might cause and rushed to get an early start. I did not encounter any delays and was checking in for my flight with our crew scheduler, and she asked if I was going out to see the pope? "I can see the pope?" I asked. "Where is he?"

"He will be boarding his flight in a few minutes. His plane is parked just in front of the one you are going out on. Go out on the ramp and watch him board," she suggested.

At this time no jetways existed at Anchorage International Airport, you just walked out across the tarmac to your plane. When I went outside I saw a red carpet and a gold rope leading to the pope's plane. I walked over and could see a crowd of people inside the terminal hovering around the door. The only person out on the tarmac, I became a little nervous until a man came out and went to the pope's plane checking inside and out before heading back inside. Soon the terminal door opened, and a figure in white emerged as I waited outside the ropes that lined his path. As he walked toward me, I suddenly realized what a unique situation I was in. It was just the pope and I together on the tarmac. The day was gray, yet the dim light gleamed off his pristinely white robe. He moved with a graceful peacefulness, and I realized I did not know the proper way to address him; His Holiness, Your Grace, Father, I just didn't know. When he reached me, he slowed, warmly smiled and nodded. Our eyes met, and I instantly felt a calming lightness, a sense of peace and grace. His eyes reflected a sincere love and acceptance that left me speechless. I stood mesmerized as he passed by, and watched the breeze ruffle the silken fabric of his robe. Before entering his aircraft, he turned, and from the top of the stairs, blessed me with the sign of the cross, nodded again, and disappeared from my view.

This encounter with Pope John Paul II affected me deeply and left me wondering what the feeling of lightness I had experienced was. He was just a man, after all. I do feel that there was something very special about him, however, and was not surprised to hear in 2014 he was canonized as a saint. I don't know about miracles, but I do know that this was an extraordinary person with an overwhelming charisma.

THE ADVENTURE CONTINUES

Early in 1978 we purchased yet another house in Anchorage. A contractor friend of Mark's had built the house and run out of money just before completion. He wanted to unload the house as soon as possible and made Mark an offer he couldn't refuse. We packed up our homey little Blackberry Street house and moved into this new, less then cozy, bigger than we needed, house. The house was a split-level, meaning when you entered, you either went up or down. The lower level is typically set partially into the ground, giving it a basement-like feel. What was unique about this house was that it was all above ground, making it unusually tall. Mark went to work finishing the garage and the landscaping, while we settled in.

Soon after Mark finished the house, (all except the sauna in the downstairs bathroom that we finished the day we moved out), he announced he was offered a job out in the "bush". Ever since we had been in Alaska, I knew that he had fantasized about working on the pipeline, or out in the villages. Not only were these jobs a once-in-a-lifetime opportunity to make some incredible money, the lure of living for a time in a remote, secluded native village, or pipeline pump station camp, attracted him. We discussed it and decided he should take the opportunity, and he signed up for a six-month commitment. I would stay home and work, take care of the house, and manage the civilized part of our lives.

Mark's new job consisted of building schools in two remote villages, Good News Bay, on the Bering Sea, and Quinhagak, some forty-five miles inland from Good News. He would fly on Wien Air Alaska to Bethel, and then catch an air taxi to Good News, if and when the weather allowed. Once out there, the crew would live among the Alaska natives, sleep in trailers, and battle the elements. The smallness of the villages caused Mark and his fellow workers to ponder the reality that they were building multi-million-dollar, state-of-the-art schools for a handful of students.

They started their projects in January, which presented all kinds of weather-related challenges: lighting, keeping the equipment from freezing, and surviving physically in this harsh environment. They had their meals and slept in trailers, and soon became friendly with the local natives. For lack of anything else to do, being so isolated, without any television or telephone, Mark began spending his evenings with the native men in their sweat lodge. The Alaska native sweat lodge is their version of a sauna, but with more water. The men gather in the excessively hot lodge (many have burn scars) and do what men do, tell stories, see who could withstand the hottest temperatures, and pass the evening. Mark began to get accustomed to the native lifestyle and appreciated the stress-free environment. After a while, he fit right in.

On the rare occasion when he was able to get a call through to me, the conversations would be less then intimate. The call came from a type of radio accessible to all the villages throughout the service area. Everyone listened in over their radio to all calls made to town. I suppose it entertained them, but it made calls uncomfortable for us to say the least. Mark came home only once during the six months, and when the projects were completed, he worried about returning to city life. If it hadn't been for me being in town, he might have stayed out there indefinitely, enjoying the challenges, and rewards of conquering them.

One of Mark's prized possessions is the pair of walrus tusks that he brought home from Good News Bay. One of the natives gave him the tusks, which are four feet long and still attached to the skull, from a legally hunted walrus. It has been his plan to one day mount them in our family room. That will only happen over my dead body. We have never had, or never will have, a game room. The tusks remain in the attic.

One night while Mark was working out in the bush, I woke up with my bed shaking. I thought it was an earthquake, but then noticed lights flashing outside my window. Our tall house swayed, and I could hear things banging into it. I got up to look outside and was horrified to see that the wind bent trees in half, random items flew through the air, and our six-foot fence was totally gone. The flashing light was lightning streaking all around, and the house continued to sway and jerk. I was terrified being home alone. The power was out, but the nonstop lightning illuminated my path as I crept into the living room. The large limbs of our mature birch trees slammed into the dining room window, and I expected them to come crashing in with the wind and rain at any moment. I looked out the front window to see if I could see any signs of life. Just as I contemplated running across the street to the neighbors, a large metal storage building went somersaulting down the street. I decided going outside would be more dangerous than staying in, even with the house under siege. I hunkered down in my bed with the blankets pulled over my head and prayed.

The storm had passed through Good News Bay, and Mark knew it was heading toward Anchorage, building strength as it traveled. With no way to contact me, Mark could only hope we were better prepared than they were. They had the framing for the second large school complex up and were ready for the next phase when the storm hit. Somehow they were able to brace the walls and keep the structure from getting blown away. To Mark's credit as a builder, of all the schools being built in the villages along the storm's path, the one he was working on was the only one to survive the ninety-mile-an-hour winds.

By morning, (ironically April Fools' Day), the winds had ceased and the sun shone on a ravaged city. Roofs blown off, fences down, and items strewn all over town. I surveyed our property and was relieved to see the only damage was the fence that was completely gone. I had never experienced anything like a hurricane before, and I hope I never do again, especially when I am home alone.

BUILDING OUR ALASKAN HOME

Mark was back working in town by summer, sixty-hour work weeks, and still making great money. I began picking up extra flights while Mark was away, and continued to do so even when he got home. That is what everyone did at that time in Alaska, taking advantage of all the work, and making lots of money. About this time we started thinking about building ourselves a home from the ground up. Neither of us had warmed to the tall split-level, and thought if we built, we could have everything just how we wanted it. We found a building lot in a new development, purchased it, and planned to begin construction the following spring. Mark already had an idea of what he wanted to build. Mostly like-minded, the plan came together over the winter. It would be a two-story, with four bedrooms, two-and-a-half baths, two large stone fireplaces, wooded lot, and everything we had always dreamed of for our home. However, we had not built a home together, and we would soon find out that we were not always so like-minded.

By spring the plans were completed, the building loan was in place, and was to be paid off by November 1st. We were both working long hours, but hey, the days were getting longer, and we figured we could work on the house at night, and on Mark's one day off each week. I had more time off, so I could run errands, check on subcontractors and deliveries. Dave, Mark's college-age brother, came up for the summer to help with our building project. Haines Construction, Inc. was also born that summer. Even though Mark still worked out of the Carpenters' Union, he decided this would be a good time to start his own construction company. The "Haines Construction, Inc., General Contractor" sign went up in front of our house in progress, and people started to take notice. Contractors started to stop by, as the area was growing, and Mark started bidding the framing on other new houses in the development.

As the summer wore on, the project progressed well, but we began to feel the November deadline looming. It was time to start choosing bathroom and kitchen finishes, lighting fixtures, flooring, etc. This is when the problems began. Mark had this questionable (to me) idea of putting wood on the ceilings. We had seen this around Anchorage, and Mark thought it very Alaskan and rugged-looking. I thought it fine for a cabin or rustic décor, BUT WE WERE NOT BUILDING A CABIN! He insisted that he wanted wood on the ceiling. It is the one thing he was adamant about. I was just as adamant that I hated wood on the ceiling, insisting that it would not go with the elegant design of our house. We agreed on the bathroom fixtures, countertops, appliances, and flooring, but when it came time to choose lighting fixtures, we came to another standoff. It appeared that we had two different visions of what our home was to be like. When I arrived at the lighting store, Mark was already there and directed me over to a fixture he had already picked out for our dining room. “Are you kidding me? You can’t be serious. This fixture belongs in a farm house.” I exclaimed. No, he was dead serious; he actually thought this farmhouse light fixture would look good in our formal dining room. I was aghast!

“What do you want to put in the dining room?” he asked. I showed him what I had in mind, and he absolutely vetoed my choice. Because of time constraints, we had to place our order that day, so we compromised somewhere between farmhouse and chateau. I wasn’t happy about having to compromise, but what could I do? We still had the issue of whether we would put wood on the ceilings to resolve.

The interior doors and windows were being installed and we decided on a golden oak finish for the trim and cabinets. With winter being so long and dark, we stayed away from dark wood. The light oak, with a glossy lacquer finish, gave the house a classy and elegant feel. The moment of truth was upon us: Were we going to put wood on the ceiling?

The entryway, living room, and dining room were all under a high vaulted ceiling. The living room had a fireplace with natural stone reaching all the way up to the peak of the vault. This was the ceiling in question. Once Mark explained that the ceiling would be done in the same light oak with a high gloss lacquer finish, I began to reconsider. It was such a high ceiling and very dramatic when you entered through the front door. "Maybe the oak would be eye catching," I thought.

I slept on it that night and decided to give Mark the go-ahead on the ceiling finish. Excited, he went right to work. By now it was October and we had leased the split-level to be taken over by the tenants on November 1st. The days were getting shorter, and the weather was drizzly and cold. It was my goal to have the house completed before we moved in. The saying, "A carpenter's house is never finished" played over and over in my mind. I knew it would be a battle getting Mark to finish anything left undone once we moved in (The sauna in the split-level still wasn't finished, and we were about to move out). The last major project on the new house was the ceiling.

Once the wood was up, I had to admit it looked pretty good. Mark was going to put the lacquer (the old toxic kind that they don't sell anymore) on this expansive, high ceiling using a large electric spray gun and really tall ladders. By now we were rushing to get as much done as we could. Mark had sprayed one coat and decided it needed another. It was getting cold and dark, but we had to finish the ceiling that night. All the doors and windows were closed to keep the cold air from fogging the lacquer, and once the second coat was on, Mark noticed some flat spots and proceeded to touch them up. By now, with the house closed up, the effects from the lacquer began to take hold. I got dizzy and lightheaded. Mark was wearing a respirator mask, so I assumed he was okay.

Once his touch-up was done, he was still not happy (He tends to be a perfectionist), and announced he would spray the entire ceiling again. I had to get some air, so I went outside and watched through the window, shivering in the drizzle. Mark sprayed and sprayed and eventually came down to admire his work. I went in to inspect and was astounded at the beauty of the ceiling. I found Mark attempting to gather the electrical cords, fumbling around like a drunk. He began to laugh and stumble. I went to steady him and realized he was as high as a kite from the fumes! I had to get him out of there. It was late and I made the decision that the ceiling was now complete. Mark still laughed hysterically, as I maneuvered him out to the car. I began to laugh at him, making it all the harder to "pour" him into the passenger seat. We drove home with him laughing and slurring his words and just having the best time! It took an effort on my part to get him undressed and in bed, where he immediately passed out. Looking down at him sleeping with a stupid grin on his face, I worried that he may have some permanent brain damage.

The next morning, he was fine, and we went to inspect the ceiling. Amazingly, it was perfect! Spectacular! Whenever anyone entered that house, his or her first comment was always, "Wow, what a beautiful ceiling!"

We finished the house with no time to spare and began the process of moving. The new house was only a few miles from the split-level, so back and forth we drove, with loads of our belongings. We cleaned and prepared the split-level for our tenants, and had just enough time for Mark to finish the sauna. The very last night we had possession of the house, we decided to try out the now completed sauna. It was really nice, and we kicked ourselves for not finishing it while we lived there. As I said, "A carpenter's house is never finished."

Our new home was everything we had hoped it would be. Mark made sure everything was the best quality, and it showed. A lovely home to start our family in, warm, whisper-quiet, and oh so comfortable, we loved every day we spent there.

The house we built in 1975.

HAINES CONSTRUCTION, INC.

That first winter we spent in our new home was the winter Mark gave up working as a union carpenter, and devoted himself full time to building Haines Construction, Inc. He had won the framing contracts for a few houses in our growing neighborhood, and with his signs, continued to attract new business. He hired a couple of carpenters he had met on union jobs, and the company was off the ground. This particular winter was also a really cold, clear winter. Our radio alarm would go off about 5:30 a.m. with the weather report. "It's 25 degrees below zero this morning. Rise and shine." Mark would get up and eat breakfast, put layers and layers of clothes on, and head out to frame houses. I think he liked the challenge of battling the elements. One morning, right after our alarm went off, the phone rang. It was Pat, who was to become Mark's top foreman. "Mark, it's 30 below this morning. Are we working?"

"Of course we are working." Mark replied. "Why wouldn't we be working?"

When I was in town, I would drive by the job on my way out of the neighborhood, and see them on the icy, slippery roof, hindered by their layers of clothes, heavy gloves, and hats. Thick, white, rubber, military-issue "bunny boots" covered their feet. These comical looking boots were purchased at the army surplus store and worn by anyone working outdoors in subzero temperatures. I have no idea how they got anything done in all that cold weather gear, but they did.

Wien Air Alaska had been expanding to destinations in the Lower 48, or the contiguous United States. This was a welcome change for me, allowing for mini vacations from the long winter. Some trips were two days, and some were three. Phoenix was a favorite, even though we were there for only one night. We would leave Anchorage very early wrapped in our down jackets and boots and arrive in time to sit outside in our hotel courtyard, smelling the orange blossoms, while being caressed by the warm desert air. We would stay outside too late, but still feel revitalized the next morning as we headed back to below zero temperatures.

Another favorite schedule of mine was our flight to Salt Lake City, Utah. We would start with a 6:30 a.m. (5:30 a.m. check-in) departure to Kodiak Island, and then back to Anchorage. The next leg from Anchorage was the three-and-a-half hour flight to Seattle, and then on to Spokane. From there on to Boise, ending up in Salt Lake City about 10 p.m., tired and hungry from this really long day. The return flight left the next morning before the crew had the FAA required rest time. Consequently, we got to spend two nights in Salt Lake with an entire day off. With the limited shopping options we had in Anchorage, we became like kids in a candy store. We would have breakfast in bed, spend most of the afternoon shopping, and then go out for a nice dinner and return home the next day. With these long days of flying, we got our monthly hours, completing this trip five times a month - ten days of flights, and five days of shopping. I loved this schedule and worked it quite often. It was a great job: My coworkers, diverse and adventurous, the pay quite good (we were among the highest paid flight attendants in the world), and you just never knew what experiences awaited, or whom you might meet. We used to ask each other if we liked our jobs, and the response would always be, "Beats working."

The oil-rich state continued to boom. Mark's company grew and already produced sizable profits. Our real estate portfolio also grew. Over a period of time we purchased two apartment buildings. Together with the houses and duplex we already owned, we managed about twenty-five rental units. With me being gone for days at a time, helping with Haines Construction, Inc. when I was in town, and Mark working long hours managing his multiple job sites, we were burning the candle at both ends. We did get management in place for the apartments, but managed the other units ourselves. It all sounds exhausting to me now, but we were young, and that is what everyone was doing in Alaska at that time, working long hours and making money.

We did take some time off to enjoy the fruits of our labors. Together with friends we went out to expensive dinners, traveled when we could get away, usually in winter, and bought pretty much anything we wanted. Life was good considering we were still in our twenties.

TRAVEL

Mark tends to have a one-track mind. When he is working, he is all in. If there are jobs available, he is doing them. The problem, at least for me, was that there was an endless supply of jobs in Anchorage, and we had airline passes! He managed to break away during the winter for an occasional sun break to Hawaii, and we usually went home to California for Christmas and New Year's, but the rest of the time, the passes burned a hole in my pocket!

My schedule was flexible, because I could trade trips with my fellow flight attendants. As long as I got the required rest between trips, I could move all of my flight days to the first half of the month, and then be off the second half. I could have taken a trip every month if I wanted to. There were always packages offered to flight crews at ridiculously low prices. I would bring a brochure home to show Mark, such as, a week in Japan including roundtrip airfare, hotels and tours, all for eighty dollars. What? Eighty dollars? Are you kidding? Mark's response would be that he was too busy, and that he needed my assistance with the business, too. After a while, I decided I was not going to miss these opportunities and booked the Japan trip with a fellow flight attendant (her husband was too busy also). The trip was fabulous, and when I returned home with pictures and stories, I could tell that Mark was sorry he hadn't gone. He did try to put a guilt trip on me, with sad stories about how much he struggled without his "girl Friday." I tried to explain to him that he needed to find a balance and take time to enjoy life, but to no avail. He went back to work.

My airline pass benefits also included my parents. They took advantage and came to Alaska several times, traveled to see family, and enjoyed this opportunity for free travel. I regularly perused my Interline Magazine to see what deals were being offered to crew members, and I noticed an offer to travel to Tahiti that allowed you to bring siblings for the same next-to-nothing price. I called my sister who lived in South Lake Tahoe, CA, and asked her if she wanted to go to Tahiti for eighty dollars, including roundtrip airfare from Los Angeles and seven nights' accommodations. Who would turn down an offer like that? Well, Mark did, but other than him I can't think of anyone. With Mark pouting the whole time, Julie jumped at the opportunity, and we devised a plan to meet in Los Angeles, with her traveling from Lake Tahoe, and me from Anchorage. We planned to spend the night, go to Disneyland the next day, and then catch our midnight flight out of LAX. Early April, Tahoe and Anchorage were still in a deep freeze, so we were both looking forward to the tropical South Pacific. After a tiring day of travel, we rendezvoused at our designated hotel and spent the evening catching up and settling in for a good rest before our all night-flight the following night.

Neither one of us had been to Disneyland, nor anywhere like it, in several years. With the warm southern California sunshine on our backs, a light midweek crowd in the park, we rode every ride, went to every show, and ate all the junk food we could stomach, until time to head to the airport for our midnight flight. I have never been able to sleep on an airplane. Even after that long day at Disneyland, I squirmed and shifted in my small, coach-cabin seat the entire night. Back then we did not have personal entertainment centers, or even a movie on the overhead screen that I can remember. Julie did not sleep either, and we both sighed with relief when we landed in Papeete on the island of Tahiti at 7:00 a.m., local time. However, when we stepped off the airplane, the oppressive heat and humidity covered us like a heavy blanket.

We were not prepared for what we encountered at the Papeete airport. No air-conditioning, uniformed officers patrolling with automatic weapons strapped over their shoulders, and no English signage. The first leg of our trip was on the neighboring island of Bora Bora, and we had to find our connecting flight. Hot, tired, cranky and disoriented, we both questioned our decision to travel to this muggy, sticky place. We found a board showing departing flights and retrieved our tickets from our bags, only to discover our reservations were for a flight at 5:00 p.m. Ten hours to wait in this sweltering airport with nowhere to rest or get something cool to drink! We were wilting fast. Julie took charge and went to try to communicate with one of the ticket agents, and miraculously got us on a flight leaving immediately. I don't know why we were not booked on that flight to begin with, but we rushed out to the six-seat island hopping plane as our bags were being loaded, thanking the good Lord for giving us northerners a break.

The plane was cramped, but at least cool. Being in such close quarters gave us each good access to a window for taking in the scenery. Once airborne, the sleepless night and heavy heat conspired with the rolling movement of the aircraft to bring on nausea. We both felt it, and glancing at Julie, I wondered if my face glowed as green as hers. Soon we were high enough to get a bird's eye view of the vividly colored South Pacific, and were able to forget the motion sickness as we spotted small islands and began our first decent to the island of Huahine. Unfortunately, we could only stick our heads out of the airplane door to get a glimpse of the airport and surrounding area. I felt a little disappointed that even though we were on the island, I would probably never be back with time to explore it. My disappointment was short lived as we buckled in for our final destination, Bora Bora!

As we descended and the island came into view, we were mesmerized by the stunning array of the ocean's blues and greens. I also noted what appeared to be a collection of islands surrounding the lush, mountainous main island. I had not educated myself on the geography of Tahiti and Bora Bora beforehand (there was no internet in those days), so I was confused when we landed on one of the outlying islands instead of the main one. A small tourist bus whisked away the other four passengers, as we waited for someone to greet us. We went into what served as the terminal for this local, one-landing-strip airport, and an agent greeted us, advising in limited English that our bus would be here momentarily. There was nothing in the terminal except a small counter for the ticket agent, and a wire rack of less-than-appealing-looking candy and chips. As we waited, the empty airplane we arrived on took off, leaving us feeling somewhat…stranded.

By now, nearing midday, the sun blazed in a clear, deep blue sky. All I could think about was reaching our air-conditioned room, where I planned to stretch out for a restorative nap. Soon a van pulled up, and the French speaking driver escorted us outside and loaded our bags. As we climbed inside, we immediately realized the van was not air-conditioned. We exchanged glances, sharing the hope we would not have far to go. We followed an unpaved road between thick growths of palms, ferns, and unrecognizable trees and shrubs for about half a mile and arrived at our hotel, a collection of small huts situated in a circle on the beach with a main building at one end. We dragged ourselves inside to check in, and our faces fell as it was no cooler inside. *How do these people live in this oppressive heat with no air-conditioning*, we wondered.

After checking in, the receptionist gave us a tour of the grounds, restaurant, and beach, explaining that we were on part of a barrier reef, and the main part of the island, where all the hotels and restaurants were located - except ours - was across the lagoon. "Can we get there from here?" we asked. He explained there was a ferry that went round-trip on the days a flight came in with tourists. Our hut, which was not beach-front, but steps away, was quite charming, with wood floors, and a sliding door leading to a deck that opened to tropical gardens. The shower was open air, and palm fronds were to become a part of our showering experience. If it weren't so miserably hot, it would have been perfection. When we asked about air-conditioning, our guide pointed out the ceiling fan and opened the sliding door. After explaining that breakfast was served in the restaurant at 8 a.m., lunch at 1 p.m., and dinner at 8 p.m., he left us to settle in.

After a failed attempt to take a nap in the heat of the afternoon, we decided to have a look around. The courtyard gardens were lovely, and there was a ping-pong table and other amusements for the guests. This was notable as there were no televisions, radios, or even telephones in the rooms. We had not even seen a newspaper, or any connection to the outside world at all. We had not seen any other guests and attempted to occupy ourselves with a game of ping pong. Within a few minutes, sweat dripped into our eyes, obscuring our vision, and we tossed our paddles aside and made our way back to our hut to get our swimming suits. "I really don't want to stay here for five nights, do you?" Julie asked as we reached our hut. Neither of us wanted to swelter in the oppressive heat, and both felt despondent.

"It is so dead here, and so hot. I don't know what we will do here for five days," I replied. "Maybe we can call the tour company and change our itinerary."

"Let's take a swim to cool off, and then go up to the office and ask to use the phone," Julie suggested. It sounded like a good plan to me, and we headed to the beach for a refreshing swim.

The beach at the hotel was more like a lake shore. No waves at all, just the gentle lapping of warm, crystal clear water on the sand. The barrier reef surrounding the main island created a calm, protected lagoon, where the vivid bright colors forced us to squint until our eyes adjusted. Across the lagoon, the dramatic view of the lush, volcanic peaks of Bora Bora reached into the turquoise sky, and we quietly stood and let the water cool our feet, taking it all in. The soothing water and breathtaking view began to work its magic.

Our dip into the South Pacific Ocean was just what the doctor ordered. It did revive us, cooling our body temperatures. As stunning as the setting was, we still did not know what we would do there for five days, and we made our way to the office to see about changing our itinerary. "Can I help you? Are you finding everything you need?" asked the receptionist who had shown us around earlier.

"Yes, may we use your telephone?" I asked. The young man cocked his head and furrowed his brows, as if not understanding the question.

"Telephone? There is no telephone here," he stated.

"But there must be a phone somewhere," I replied. "What if there is an emergency and someone needs medical help?"

"There is a radio transmitter at the airport, but there are no more flights today so no one is there. Do you have an emergency?"

"No, no emergency, we just wanted to call our tour company."

We walked across the grounds, contemplating the fact that there would be no change of itinerary, and resigned ourselves to make the best of the next five days. Now that we had cooled off, we decided to take a rest until time to get ready for dinner.

By 7:00 p.m. we were starving. We headed up to the restaurant to have a cocktail before dinner. I do love a good tropical drink with fruit juices and rum. There were actually people in the restaurant, so we assumed there were at least a few other guests staying there. We ordered dinner from the three choices on the menu, with a bottle of wine to go with it, and enjoyed our drinks while we waited for our meal. When the waiter brought our dinners, we thought he had made a mistake. They were not what we had ordered. Then he brought us a bottle of white wine when we had ordered red. We tried explaining to him that this was not what we ordered, but he keep nodding and smiling at us so we decided to just go with the flow and enjoy the meal, whatever it was. After our dinner and bottle of wine we meandered back to our hut. The night air was warm and balmy and I felt the stress begin to ease from my shoulders as I contemplated a good night's sleep.

As we neared the step to the entrance of our hut, we heard a scratching, clacking, disturbance near the step and jumped back. With the help of my handy, dandy flashlight, we discovered two good-sized crabs battling it out for the hole under our front step. They snapped and clawed at each other mercilessly as we watched in horror. We jumped over them and went inside and shut the door. We were both a little freaked out, not being very familiar with crabs' behavior. As we prepared for bed, the clacking and fighting continued outside the door. There was a gap under our door, and we worried the crabs may get in during the night. After a time, the racket died down, and we settled in to get some sleep. Even though we had the overhead fan, it was still overly warm, and we couldn't get comfortable. We decided to be brave and opened our sliding door, crabs and all, and finally found the sleep we so needed.

I woke the next morning to the sound of birds chirping and singing. Glancing out the sliding door, a vividly colored tropical bird hopping around on our deck instantly enchanted me. I reached over and nudged Julie so we could enjoy this rare sight together. As we watched this peaceful scene, I noticed that all of our tension and stress seemed to have left us, and I thought to myself, "I could get used to this." We checked our watches, remembering that if we wanted breakfast, we had to get to the restaurant, as it was nearing 8:00 a.m. Mindful of the crabs from last night, we poked our heads out our door, and all was quiet. Each evening, however, the fight was on in front of our hut. By the second night one of the crabs had lost its claw on one side and could only maneuver in a circle. It wasn't looking good for him, but he hung in there, determined to claim the home under our step for his own. On about the fourth morning we found the remains of the losing crab, mutilated and dismembered. At least we wouldn't have to listen to the sounds of crabs attacking each other any longer; however, whenever we entered or left our hut for the remainder of our stay, we took a wide step over the crab burrow, knowing the victorious crab lurked within.

PARADISE FOUND

It took a day or two for us to unwind and adjust to the heat and humidity, but with the ocean steps away, and the realization there was nothing to do but relax, that is exactly what we did. Without the distraction of television, telephones, traffic and crowds, we began to notice the birds, the fish, visible in the crystal clear water, and even the unique insects. We met a group of two couples from Texas staying at the resort on the beach. They were friendly enough, but were the only other guests we had seen so far. They informed us that the kayaks and outriggers on the beach were there for our use, and that the snorkeling was supposed to be exceptional at the small island just across the water from our beach.

Julie asked, "Do you know how to handle an outrigger?" Being from Lake Tahoe, she had some experience.

"Not really," I replied. "But how hard can it be?"

After lunch we secured snorkeling gear, pushed one of the outriggers into the water, and climbed in. "I will paddle going over and you can paddle on the way back," Julie announced.

"Fine," I said. The water seemed calm, and I did not foresee any problems. We glided along what felt and looked like air. The water was so clear we could see the sandy, coral-dotted bottom, and all of the tropical sea-life in-between. Julie stopped rowing, and we leaned over the side, watching the vividly colored fish as clearly as if they floated in air. We really did not need the snorkeling gear with water this clear, but we continued to the island as planned.

When we arrived, the island was over-grown and we had a hard time finding a spot to beach the outrigger. Eventually we shoved it up in the bushes, put on our masks, and jumped in. The current running between these two small islands rushed quite strongly, requiring us to swim against it the entire time we were in the water. And we saw far less sea life. We declared our outrigger excursion was a bust, and proceeded to drag the outrigger out of the bushes. With me in control we headed back to our private retreat.

Well, this is not as easy as it looks, I thought as we headed back, making far slower progress than on the way over. "I think we are going against the current. Just keep rowing, we will get there," Julie encouraged.

It was a struggle getting across the inlet, fighting the current with my limited canoeing skills, but as we neared our resort I felt relieved, spotting our Texan friends just up ahead on the beach. As we got closer, the current changed again and was pushing us back out. The shore was right there in front of us, but the harder I worked the oars, the farther away we got. Julie began directing me, but despite my best efforts, we went in circles, while the shore got further and further away. The Texans laughed their heads off as we were only about thirty to forty yards off the beach, but we couldn't seem to make any headway. We continued to move away from shore as we spun around and around. Finally, with the bow of the outrigger facing the wrong way, I begged Julie to take over. From her reclining position in the outrigger she reminded me of our deal that I was in charge of rowing on the way back. She had done her part on the way over. I continued to struggle with the oars but could not get us turned around. She finally took pity on me and advised me to reverse my stroke, and to the applause and cheers of our Texan audience, we backed right onto the beach. They thanked us for the afternoon's entertainment, and I told them I had meant to impress them with my backwards rowing. Julie and I were relieved to have our snorkeling expedition over with.

After the outrigger experience, we decided to stay on dry land for a while and go exploring. We headed down the road that brought us from the airstrip and, as we stepped, the ground on either side of us crackled and snapped. As we moved, the clacking moved with us. We soon discovered that we were on an island covered with crabs. I don't know if it was mating season for them or what, but they were everywhere. They would run away if we got near (hence the clacking sound) so they didn't bother us, but it was a little unnerving knowing crabs covered the ground off the roads and trails. Whenever we reminisce about the trip to Tahiti, we refer to Bora Bora as Crab Island.

After a couple of days relaxing in the slow pace of the island, we realized we were really enjoying ourselves. The setting was truly spectacular, and we were getting used to the tropical weather, so we decided it was time to go exploring. "Maybe we can hike completely around this island," Julie suggested. "It doesn't seem very big."

"Let's give it a try. I don't think we can get lost if we follow the coastline," I added. We talked late into the night with our patio door open to the ocean breeze, enjoying what we thought we didn't want to do - nothing - until we finally drifted off to sleep.

We woke late the next morning realizing we had missed breakfast. Nothing we could do about it now, we decided we might as well head out on our hike. We walked in one direction along the beach when we could, and on dirt roads and foot trails when there was no beach. We did not see another person the entire day, but we did happen upon some fabulous white sand beaches, where we would stop and take a cooling swim, a lot of spectacular tropical plant life, and the ever present crabs, which we avoided at all costs. Eventually we came to an overgrown jungle area that we could not find our way around. Since the sun was getting low, we decided we better turn back. Besides, we were getting really hungry with all the hiking and swimming, and no breakfast or lunch.

By the time we reached our beach hut, it was late afternoon, but still several hours until dinner, and we had nothing to eat and nowhere to buy anything. I remember a fellow flight attendant who had taken this trip right before us telling me to bring snacks - because if you miss a meal, you are out of luck. "Bring a few cans of Spam," she told me. *Spam*, I thought. *I am not bringing Spam*. I thought she was nuts. *Who eats Spam?* I should have taken her advice; we could have eaten a few cans of Spam that afternoon. We were really hungry.

"Let's go outside and find something to do to keep our minds off our stomachs," I suggested." As we left our hut, we noticed one of the resort employees out among the palms with a giant machete type of sword, swinging away. We went to investigate and found he was opening coconuts for the restaurant or bar. We asked if we could have some coconut, but he didn't understand, gathered up his coconuts, and left. We moseyed around for a while, but our hunger distracted us, and we went back inside to lie down and save our energy.

About to doze off, I realized Julie had just gone outside. When she didn't come right back, I got up, stepped outside the hut, and there she was, in the palm grove, swinging that machete with everything she had. Apparently, hunger does strange things to people. I walked into the palm grove, and lo and behold she had split open a big, beautiful, ripe coconut. She chopped it into pieces, put down the machete, gathered the pieces up and brought them inside as if this were an everyday occurrence. We made quick work of the coconut meat, which was surprisingly refreshing for being unsweetened, and we were saved from starvation. I was glad that day that my sister is a mountain woman.

My sister, Julie, splitting coconuts on Bora Bora.

MORE TRIPS

Our friend Patti was going to be in New York City on business one summer, and asked if I wanted to get a pass and join her there. I decided to go, and we asked Mark if he wanted to join us. At first he refused, but then changed his mind, and we met Patti at our hotel, the legendary Waldorf Astoria. None of us had been to the Big Apple, and coming from Alaska, it was overwhelming. Once we got our bearings, we proceeded to see and do everything the city is famous for. We visited the famous delicatessens, the chocolate shops, shopped at Bloomingdales and Saks Fifth Ave. We took a helicopter sightseeing excursion and got a birds-eye view of Central Park, the Statue of Liberty, the Empire State Building, and the twin towers of the World Trade Center. At night we went to Broadway plays and then to local bars for a cocktail or a coffee shop for dessert. Our favorite play was Woman of the Year, staring the talented and stunningly beautiful Raquel Welch. I thought Mark's eyes would pop out of his head when she came out on stage in a clingy, jersey knit dress, with what appeared to be nothing underneath. By coincidence, we saw her after the play at the stage door, where she graciously greeted her fans and signed autographs.

Another night, as we meandered down Broadway, we noticed a group of people up ahead of us. As we neared we realized it was the boxing champion of the time, Muhammad Ali. No autographs or pictures were obtained by any of us, which I do regret, but as Alaskans, we were not as impressed by the rich and famous, as others may have been. But it was neat to see him on the street.

FIGI

Roundtrip flights to Fiji, ten days split between two resorts, meals, tours, and all, once again, for next to nothing. Mark began to realize he should take advantage of these fabulous travel opportunities, and we made our reservations and started packing. Neither of us had been to the Fijian Islands, but knowing it would be balmy and sunny in February was all we needed to know. We left Anchorage on the red-eye bound for Hawaii and then on to Nadi, on Fiji's largest island, Viti Levu (Big Fiji), to spend a couple of nights.

Once again the extreme change in climate shocked our systems. Boarding our aircraft in Anchorage at five degrees below zero, and stepping off in humid, sticky Nadi, shifted our metabolisms into low, slow gear. Where was the water, a swimming pool, the ocean, or anyplace with air-conditioning? Ten days was not enough time to adjust to a climate change such as this, and a sensible person would have monitored their heat and sun exposure. However, good sense is not something northerners bring along on their winter escapes. We were driven by our need for sunlight and warmth.

Our first days at a nice enough resort outside of Nadi were somewhat uncomfortable, with no air-conditioning, and that thick, heavy air. Not to mention the geckos climbing the walls in our room. I'm sorry, but I could not sleep with these reptiles slinking around in my personal space. What if they jumped or fell on me during the night? When I requested they be removed from our room, the staff assured me they were harmless and would eat mosquitoes or other pests that might disturb us during our stay. If his logic was supposed to reassure me, it didn't. I was on Gecko alert any time I was in my room.

Our hotel in Nadi, or Nandy, as it is sometimes spelled (we never understood why there were two spellings) was not very interesting. It could have been the jet lag and heat, but we spent the time winding down and just relaxing. On the third day we embarked by bus to our main destination down the Coral Coast. My tendency to suffer motion sickness while dealing with exhaust fumes, windy roads, and humidity, made the ride less than enjoyable. There wasn't much to see from the road, but upon arrival I immediately perked up as we entered through lushly landscaped grounds, into the elegant and open lobby, looking out to the glistening ocean, and then to our thankfully air-conditioned room. After a brief rest in our cool and comfortable suite at our destination resort, I was ready to experience the real Fiji.

Fijians are the friendliest native people we had ever encountered, and well educated. Every one of them spoke good English. They wore very little in the way of clothing, a length of fabric wrapped from chest to knees for women and a much smaller piece wrapped from below the bellybutton to mid-thigh for men.

Even the employees of the hotel wore this traditional attire. The men, for the most part, were tall and physically fit. I had no problem with them being almost naked. Fijians are fascinated by tourists from the United States, but when they heard we were from ALASKA, they awed at our presence. At the time there was no television on the islands and no real connection to the world beyond, thus the hunger to know everything about the US, and especially the frozen northland, which the locals fantasized about visiting one day. We lounged by the pool, explored the coral reef at low tide, and partied like celebrities at night. Many of the other tourists there were from Australia and New Zealand and were also fascinated by having Alaskans in their midst.

Two days of resort life were about all Mark and I had patience for, so we signed up for an excursion to an outlying island. The day included snorkeling at a spectacular coral reef and visiting a native village. The boat was sleek and fast, with a dozen or so tourist soaking up the sun and the endless shades of blue. Flying fish, which do appear to fly, accompanied and entertained us along the way. We anchored off shore of a small, natural island paradise to explore the reef that surrounded it, and meet the island's inhabitants. We all donned the provided snorkels and masks and stepped off the side of the boat into the jewel colored liquid. Silky, warm water caressed my body as my eyes feasted on the multitude of shapes and colors that made up the reef and the sea life drawn to it. The contrast between the black and white of an Anchorage winter and this explosion of sensual delights nourished our sun-starved souls. All too soon the time came to visit the village.

Barely dressed natives greeted us as we emerged from the jungle path into a circle of huts comprising their homes. Children rushed to see the visitors and show us a favored toy or trinket. Our guide explained that we would be visiting the chief's hut to participate in a traditional kava ceremony and cautioned us that not finishing the offered drink would be an insult to the chief's hospitality. "No problem," I thought. I had worked up a thirst on the walk from the lagoon and was ready to get out of the hot sun. We meandered around the village, learning about the local fishing techniques and slow-paced lifestyle until the chief was ready to receive us.

The humidity became oppressive, and I ducked through the low entry into the hut expecting a little relief, only to be overwhelmed by a suffocating, sweltering fog. One wall of the hut was ablaze, as a large wood burning oven pulsed with heat. Our guide motioned for us to be seated on the floor, where I was about to end up anyway. It had to have been 130 degrees in there! There was a Canadian couple in our group and the four of us northerners were wilting like weeping willows. The chief's assistant pulled a large whitish root out of a burlap bag and wrapped it in cheesecloth. He then placed it in a large wooden bowl of water and swooshed it around for a while. Eventually he took a small bowl and filled it with the milky liquid and passed it to one of the guests, who drank it down and handed the bowl back to the assistant. Then the bowl was refilled and handed to me. With apprehension I brought it to my lips and sipped. It tasted like dirt, but what could I do? All eyes on me, I quickly drank the entire contents and handed the empty bowl back to our server, hoping I wouldn't be sorry later. After the ceremony I became entranced as the chief entertained us with island legends. As I listened, it dawned on me that the heat wasn't bothering me anymore. I guessed I'd finally adjusted to the climate.

I could have continued listening to the chief all afternoon, but story time had come to an end, and it was time to leave the village. As we stood and exited the hut I realized why I wasn't suffering from the heat anymore. I wasn't feeling much of anything at all. The whole tour group was intoxicated from the kava. We learned later kava serves not only as a ceremonial drink, but as a party beverage as well. Wow, good thing we were heading back to our boat - I was drunk. Once back on board, the ocean air, flying fish, and unsurpassed beauty revived us, and we arrived at the hotel ready to dress for dinner and the evening's nightlife.

After a refreshing shower and a little recovery time in our air-conditioned room, we headed down to dinner. The resort restaurant offered Fijian cuisine consisting of meat or fish stews, seasoned with local herbs and spices. The food was tasty enough, but the service was Fijian style, laughable compared to US standards. Slow does not describe the waiters in the restaurant. If you needed more water, you could have died of thirst before they came to refill your glass. We learned to get up and find what we needed on our own. Don't get me wrong, the hotel staff was genuinely friendly and polite. They just saw no need to rush. I spent a pleasant afternoon in my room with the housekeeper who was fascinated watching me give myself a manicure. I don't know what she was supposed to be doing, but she spent about ninety minutes sitting and chatting with me. I guessed she was on a Fijian schedule.

After dinner we made our way to the nightclub where there was live music and lots of happy, friendly Australians, who encouraged us to join them at their tables and bought us drinks, treating us as if we were honored guests. We were having a great time, drinking, dancing, laughing with our new friends, when suddenly I felt a rumbling in my stomach. *Oh no*, I thought. *This is not good.* The rumbling progressed to pain and an urgency to get to the ladies' room in a hurry. I told Mark where I was going and hurried through the lobby as I broke out in a sweat and began to feel faint.

As I pushed open the ladies' room door, the urgency overwhelmed me. I was about to be sick from both ends, but what was this? A sitting room. I stumbled to the door at the far end, only to then find myself in a room with sinks and mirrors. *Where were the toilets?* I spotted another door and raced to it and finally reached the toilets. I sat down and relieved that emergency but began to sway as the sweat continued to pour off me. Alone in these rooms, I realized I needed help, and stood to exit the stall. The next memory I have is of hearing a loud thud and then nothing. I woke up sometime later sprawled on the floor and realized the thud I remembered hearing was my head hitting the cold, hard tile. Again I knew I had to find help. I managed to get up, still feeling sick and woozy as I made my way to the door. *These doors again, how many doors does this bathroom have?* I fretted as I pushed one after another trying to get out.

The next thing I knew I was gazing up at a group of people hovering over me, all talking at once: "Is she all right?"

"Is there a doctor here?"

"Go to the desk for help."

"She's waking up. Miss, Miss, who are you here with?"

I was flat on my back on the floor of the hotel lobby. At least there was carpeting this time, I thought to myself. "My husband is in the bar. His name is Mark Haines."

Meanwhile, Mark was thinking I had been gone a long time and perked up when he heard people asking from table to table "Are you Mark Haines, are you Mark Haines?"

And then he knew I must be having a problem.

He rescued me from the lobby floor, after learning there was no doctor at the hotel, but they could send for the local doctor from the village down the road. I pictured some sort of native Fijian in a loin-cloth and decided against it. "I just want to go to bed," I told them, and thanked them for their help. I was still nauseated and weak, with a growing lump on my head, but felt if I could just get to bed I would be fine in the morning.

I slept through the night and did feel better in the morning. I was a little shaky but relieved that I had not seriously hurt myself by hitting my head on the hard tile floor. It was the combination of the extreme heat and sun on our tour, and the Fijian food and drink, not to mention the kava, that took me down, but by afternoon I was ready to continue our adventure. I now know not to stand up when I feel faint. The floor is a long way down.

We spent that afternoon swimming and exploring the tide pool, but I had become more cautious about sun exposure and getting overheated. I did not want to have another episode, so we decided we would rent a car the next day and drive to Suva, the capital of Fiji, which was about 60 miles away, and do a little duty-free shopping and exploring. That sounded safe enough.

~

The concierge tilted his head, looking at us quizzically as he asked, "Why do you want to rent a car?" We explained we wanted to visit Suva for a change of scenery.

"Well, tourists don't usually drive to Suva from here," he explained. "The road is steep and narrow, and not recommended for a pleasure drive."

We did know that in Fiji they drive on the opposite side of the road, like in England, but we felt we could handle that. "Isn't it only sixty miles? How bad can it be? We want to go ahead with the rental."

Soon we were on our way. Initially the road was fine and there was little traffic, so we turned onto the road to Suva and headed directly into the mountains. Within the next few minutes, the road turned to dirt. Not just dirt, but rocks of varying sizes. We were forced to slow down as the road narrowed to what seemed like one lane. Up we went, winding slowly towards the top, when out of nowhere, a speeding truck came roaring around the bend. Mark hugged the edge as close as possible without going off the side of the mountain, and the truck blasted by as if we weren't on the road at all. "That was scary; I hope that's the only truck we meet today!" Mark exclaimed. But as soon as we got back on the road, another one appeared and nearly pushed us off the mountain. We began to understand why tourists were discouraged from driving this road.

We proceeded as cautiously as we could, but not being able to see around the curves gave us no warning when another truck might appear. And appear they did. A steady stream of oversized trucks flew by us, throwing rocks and raising dust, hindering our visibility. "Oh my gosh! This is such a dangerous road," I said to Mark. "What should we do?"

"What can we do?" he answered. "There is nowhere to turn around so we will have to continue on. I think we are about half way - maybe it will be better going down."

Just then a speeding truck came barreling towards us, and all we could do was duck as a huge rock was kicked up by the truck and came flying right at us. It bounced off our windshield and shattered it into a thousand spider-webbed veins. The windshield stayed fixed in the frame, but it was nearly impossible to see out of. "This is just great, now we can barely see anything. This is turning into a nightmare," Mark complained. But it was about to get worse.

As we drove along, trying to see what was in front of us through the intricately webbed windshield and straining to see or hear oncoming trucks, we suddenly bounced off a boulder, and the entire windshield came raining down on us. Hundreds of pieces of glass, covering the dashboard, and our seats and laps. "Should we get out and brush some of this glass out? I am afraid we will get cut?" I asked.

"It's too dangerous to get out on this road. We could be killed by one of these trucks," Mark reasoned. "We will have to deal with this glass and keep moving. Here comes another truck. Duck!"

Now we had nothing shielding us from the flying rocks and dust as it all came at us, covering us with a layer of dirt and stinging us as tiny rocks hit us in the face. We both wished we had taken the hint from the concierge back at the hotel, but we had no option but to continue. Truck after truck raced by us, each throwing more dirt and rocks, not to mention the wind that lashed at us the entire time. At least we had sunglasses to protect our eyes.

The harrowing sixty miles took us several hours, but at long last we were descending the mountain and finally reached pavement. By now it was late afternoon, and Suva appeared to be in the midst of rush hour. "Look for an Avis Car Rental," Mark suggested. "We have to get another car. We are not driving this one back to the resort." The traffic was horrific, and driving on the opposite side confused us all the more. Amazingly I spotted an Avis sign to our left, and pointed it out to Mark. In his anxious state, he swerved into the turning lane and hit what he expected to be the blinker. With the drivers control's all on the right side, the windshield wipers were where the blinker should have been, and, shock of all shocks, the wiper blades came swishing inside almost stabbing us in the chest. Our hearts were in our throats as the wipers began to swish, swish across the dash board, sending the glass particles flying all over the car. While we attempted to survive the attack of the wiper blades and to dodge the flying glass, the light changed and the other drivers began honking and shaking their fists at us to get out of the way. Somehow, in the midst of all this chaos, Mark got the wipers turned off, got us out of the intersection and into the Avis parking lot, exhausted and stressed, but still in one piece.

We got out of the car, brushing dirt, rocks, and glass off of ourselves, and walked towards the office. Passing a large window, I saw my reflection in the glass and stopped in my tracks. My face was black except for the circles left clean around my eyes from my sunglasses. My dust-and dirt-filled hair had been sculpted by the wind into something resembling a beehive, or the style the Bride of Frankenstein wore in the movie of the same name. We looked at each other and back at our reflections and broke into a long, stress-relieving laugh at ourselves, and headed inside to find the restrooms to at least wash our hands and faces.

Avis gave us a new car, and we spent a short time looking around Suva, but really wanted to get back on the road, not knowing what the drive back would be like. Thankfully the truckers had all retired for the day, and we had a much smoother, uneventful drive back to the resort. All in all, we enjoyed our visit to Fiji, despite our misadventures. I would like to go back someday, but would heed the advice of locals and try to stay out of trouble.

Chapter 6

1983 - A REMARKABLE YEAR

Big changes were in store for us this year. We were surprised but not shocked when we learned in the fall of 1982 that I was pregnant. Even though we had planned to have a family, our life had been so full and interesting since our marriage that we kept putting it off. In the back of my mind, the biological clock ticked as I turned twenty-nine in March of 1982. I went off the birth control pill, thinking I should prepare my body for when the time came. Even though I used other methods of birth control, the time came before we even had time to form a family plan. We decided it was meant to be, and that I would be thirty when the baby came, and that it was happening, ready or not.

It was the policy at Wien Air Alaska that flight attendants went on leave-of-absence as soon as they knew they were pregnant. That was fine with me. Not feeling so well, I was delighted to have the unexpected time off. I planned to return to work once I weaned the baby at about six months, not fully understanding what being the mother of a newborn would require. We went home for Christmas with the exciting news, and both families were thrilled at the prospect of this first grandchild. We adjusted to the idea, but did not fully realize the changes this little person would bring with his arrival.

I was healthy and happy, preparing the nursery, taking Lamaze classes (natural birthing) with Mark, and I joined an exercise class for pregnant women. During the 80s, giving birth naturally was the trend. We were led to believe that pain medication, or drugs of any kind, could be harmful to the baby, and that a healthy young woman should be able to give birth easily, if she learned to breathe properly. This may be true for some woman, but I, unfortunately, was not one of the lucky ones.

~

When I was about six months along, I noticed a small mole on my check that always drew my attention. It would itch or tingle, making me think I had a mosquito bite. But when I looked in the mirror, I saw a little mole. I did not think too much about it, until I mentioned it to a friend, who told me to get it checked as soon as possible. She had had a friend with a similar spot, and within a matter of months, her friend was dead. I did not think I was near death, but I called and made an appointment with the dermatologist anyway. When I saw him the following week, he was not concerned, but removed the spot just to be safe. He told me to come back in a week for the test results. I did not give the issue any more thought until I returned to find the young, not very experienced doctor, looking pale and apprehensive. "I am sorry to have to tell you this, but the pathology report confirms malignant melanoma. We have caught it early, and I believe that with a wide excision of the area you should not have to worry about a recurrence. A plastic surgeon will do the operation as soon as we can get it scheduled. I have already spoken to him, and since you are six months pregnant, he wants to do it at the hospital."

I didn't know what to say. I knew nothing about melanoma, and was not happy about having to have surgery on my face. After a little research and talking to friends and family, the reality that melanoma is a very dangerous cancer, with no cure, unsettled my easygoing pregnancy. Further testing was put on hold until after the baby, but we were reassured that the cancer was in its first stage, and the chance that it had spread was very small. Thank goodness I mentioned that annoying little itch on my face to my friend, who had persuaded me to see a dermatologist while the cancer remained at such an early stage. I may not have had it checked without her urging.

I had the surgery, a wide excision about the size of a quarter on my right cheek, and returned home with bandages taped to my face. After a few days I took off the bandages and was horrified to see black wiry stitches forming a railroad track down my cheek. To close the wide excision, the skin was pulled so tight I had a one-sided grin, making me look like a goofball. As if the physical ravages of pregnancy weren't bad enough, now this!

After the stitches came out and my skin had time to stretch itself back into place, I was relieved that the scar healed amazingly fast, and I could put this cancer scare out of my mind and focus on getting ready for our baby.

~

1983 was our seventh year in Alaska, and Mike's mother had been right about every seventh year being unusually warm, sunny, and spectacular, like our first summer had been. It was a glorious time to be on a leave-of-absence. Mark worked long hours, as our construction company continued to grow, and I helped with paperwork, errands, or anyway I could be useful. In addition to my three-times-a-week exercise class, I took long walks every afternoon, enjoying the splendor of the early spring and long warm days of summer. When the weather is fine like it was that summer, there is nowhere more beautiful and nowhere else I would rather have been. With the long hours of sunlight, nature bursts from the mountains and valleys in vivid colors, sights, and scents. The inlet, the rivers, and lakes are all teeming with fish and sea life, and wildlife roamed freely, even in town, getting fat from the season's abundance.

~

My due date was June 26th, which came and went with no signs of labor. The shower gifts all put away, the nursery decorated, and my mother arrived to help me, but still no baby. By now I waddled around the neighborhood each afternoon, hoping the exercise would start labor, but nothing happened. I saw the doctor on Thursday, July 7th, and he said I was not showing signs of labor, and when he got back in town on Monday, we would induce labor. "What do you mean, get back in town? You're leaving?" I asked.

"I will only be gone for the weekend," he said. "I will see you first thing Monday morning. Continue your afternoon walks; it may help to start labor."

I took a long walk that afternoon hoping to start labor before he left town, but it did no good. My mother worried about my dad, who had been stricken with rheumatoid arthritis, and struggled without her help. She had not planned to be away from him for more than two weeks, and that time had come and gone. At the same time, she wanted to be with me for the birth of my first child, and see us settled before she left. Still we waited.

I walked again on Friday, despite feeling like an over-stuffed turkey, but managed to find energy from the warm sun and fresh air. I was getting on pretty well for being ten days overdue, still eating and sleeping without too many problems, so I didn't know what had awakened me about midnight, Friday night, until I realized my gown and bed were all wet. Had the pressure caused me to wet myself, I wondered? I felt I was losing control of my bodily functions. Then it dawned on me, my water had broken. I woke Mark, called the hospital, and was told to come in right away. "But I am not feeling any pains," I remarked. She said that didn't matter, the pains would be starting soon. The three of us prepared ourselves for a long night and headed out.

It was not just a long night, but a long weekend. My baby boy, Ryan, did not give up his secure, snug home until early Sunday morning. I was exhausted, and a little bitter, that after all the Lamaze classes, coaching, and reading I had done, I was totally unprepared for a difficult birth. During labor, Mark attempted the Lamaze coaching he had learned, directing me to breathe and focus until I screamed "Get out of my face! I am trying to have a baby here." Poor guy, he didn't deserve that, but I had no interest in counting short, quick breaths while my body was being taken over by aliens. Mom, who had delivered five babies quickly and easily, was beside herself watching my travails as the hours dragged on. "How long are they going to let her go on like this?" she asked the nurse. After twenty-four hours, I finally broke down and allowed myself a dose of Demerol, (which did very little) desperate for some relief.

By now it was early Sunday morning, and in walked my doctor. He had returned from his weekend excursion in time to help me end the misery. About 2 a.m., with me pushing with all the strength I had left, and the doctor actually pushing down on my stomach from the outside, Ryan Christopher Haines was born. I collapsed in exhaustion while the nurses took the baby and the doctor finished up. I heard him comment to my husband, "If I had known the baby's head was that big, I never would have let her deliver him naturally." I wondered why he didn't know - he was the doctor after all.

All the pain and agony was soon forgotten once I finally held that warm little bundle in my arms. He was so alert for a new born, looking right at me as I spoke. When Mark spoke, he turned his little head and zeroed in on him, as if he already recognized our voices. From that moment on we were enchanted. He was the most perfect baby ever born and we were determined to do our best as his parents. Mom stayed one more week to help us get baby Ryan settled at home, but she felt anxious about my dad being left alone for so long. She hated to leave her first grandchild so soon, but felt that she must. With Mom gone and Mark working long days, I learned what it means to be a mother: how to function on little to no sleep, how to do chores with one hand while cradling a baby in the other, and to accept that for the time being anyway, I had no social life. At least I didn't have to go back to work; my leave-of-absence had been extended indefinitely.

Ryan and I at bath time.

~

That memorable summer slipped away as we adjusted to our new routines. Construction continued to boom, and Anchorage was still bursting at the seams as young, adventurous cheechakos continued to arrive daily to take advantage of the rapidly growing city. In large part, they succeeded, quickly getting jobs, earning much more than they had ever imagined. It was an exciting time for everyone experiencing this unique period in history. The population consisted of the local sourdoughs, who were rugged and used to extremes. And the new, young, oil company employees, construction workers, from every state in the Lower 48, and fresh out of school professionals, opening their first offices and business. These young people (mostly men) frequented the new restaurants and shops as they came on the scene, spending the pockets full of money that everyone seemed to have. Many of them took advantage of the great outdoors when they weren't working the long hours that most of us worked. With our wonderful new home, a growing, profitable business, and our little family, leaving was the last thing on our minds.

When the holidays rolled around, we went home to California to introduce the family to six-month-old Ryan. He was the center of attention, and we were able to go out and visit friends, taking full advantage of all the babysitters. Towards the end of this visit, I got a call from Wien letting me know that I was being called back to work and expected to return January 1st. I had assumed I would be able to be off through the winter, when there was less business, but this was not the case. Mark and I had agreed that I would return to work at some point, but we had become comfortable with me at home and realized we had to quickly make arrangements for childcare. I would be gone for days at a time, so Mark would be the on-call parent during that time, business owner or not. He had been spoiled with me being the main caregiver, but he was about to find out what parenthood is all about.

My schedule that first month back to work took me to Phoenix, Arizona, where we spent the night and came home the next day. We had found a lovely young woman with a baby of her own to look after Ryan during the day. Mark would pick him up before 6:00 p.m., and care for him until the next morning. I had worried about leaving the two of them alone, but as soon as I got on the airplane, I felt as if I were on vacation. I could do my work without interruptions, converse with adults, have meals at mealtime, and soon found that I was not worrying about them at all. When we arrived in Phoenix, the weather was balmy, to us anyway; it was January, and we sat outside in the hotel courtyard, enjoying the warm air and a glass of wine. *Heaven can't be better than this,* I thought, as I looked forward to a night of uninterrupted sleep.

I returned home the next day from two long work days, feeling more refreshed and rested than I had since having the baby. I looked forward to seeing my guys, but when I arrived, I found Mark frazzled, and at his wit's end. He gave Ryan his bottle with one hand held the telephone with the other. "I am on the phone with the pediatrician's office. Take Ryan and I'll fill you in when I hang up." I reached for him and he cried out when he saw me. I hugged him to my chest, and then held him out looking for signs of illness or injury.

He looked fine and was so happy to be in his mommy's arms that I couldn't imagine what was wrong. Mark hung up and exclaimed "I am so glad you're back. We were up all night and at the doctors' this morning. I am a wreck! I don't know if this is going to work out after all."

"What's wrong?" I asked. "Everything seems fine."

"I got him to bed about 9:00 p.m. last night, but he woke me up crying about midnight. I went to check on him, and when I picked him up he was burning with fever." *Fever*? I wondered. *Ryan had not been sick at all since we brought him home from the hospital.*

"What did you do? How high was his fever?"

"It was 104 degrees. I freaked out! Of all times for him to get sick, the first night you are gone. I called the doctor, and they told me it was not a crisis and to give him baby Tylenol and a cool sponge bath, and the fever will come down. I couldn't believe they were so nonchalant about a 104-degree fever! I followed their instructions and after a cool bath, he settled down and went back to sleep. I kept him in bed with me because I was too worried to leave him alone. He slept restlessly until morning, but I didn't sleep at all. In the morning we went to the doctor and they explained that this can happen with babies, and he seems to have recovered as is usually the case. I stayed home with him, and he is eating and playing like nothing happened. He's fine, but I'm a basket case."

So, I thought, *now he knows what it means to care for a baby.* I continued to work, and that was the only time a problem arose. It was stressful for Mark when I was gone, not having the freedom to work twelve hour days if he chose, or any freedom at all for that matter. However, they adjusted to a father/son schedule, and I continued to relish my "time off" when I went to work.

Ryan checking out Dad's fresh caught king salmon.

~

Mark's construction company continued to generate generous profits, and we continued to invest in real estate. By 1984 we had sold the duplex and bought three small apartment complexes, a 12-unit, a 10-unit, and a 4-unit. In addition to the apartments, we still owned the house we had rented out when we moved into the one we built, and a parcel of land Mark planned to develop. Reliable management for this type of real estate portfolio was next-to-impossible to find. Therefore, in addition to our full time jobs - Haines Construction being more than full time, and being parents - we were hands-on property managers. Somehow we made it all work, and even found time to socialize and travel a couple of times a year. Sunshine breaks to Hawaii in winter or spring became necessary for mental stability. It perplexed us when eighteen-month-old Ryan could not comprehend being outside without shoes and socks, even at the beach. We adored our little guy and planned to have another baby soon, and before I had time to think it through, I was pregnant again.

After the initial shock, I began to plan for my little girl. I assumed it would be a girl because I really wanted a daughter, and life up to now had always turned out as I planned. Ryan would be two-and-a-half when the baby came, and I thought that was perfect timing. It was winter and I had taken a leave of absence, which was offered during Wien's slow months, so I didn't report my pregnancy right away. I was glad to be off work, though, because I was not feeling well, much worse than I had with Ryan. At only three months along I began having back aches and a general feeling that all was not well. The backaches increased, especially when I was on my feet, so I went to the doctor and he ordered an ultrasound. The baby measured the size of a nine-week-old, but I was at least twelve weeks. I exclaimed to the technician that there must be a mistake, but she assured me there was no mistake; the baby measured nine weeks. The doctor explained that it appeared the baby had died and stopped growing at nine weeks, and my body was trying to miscarry, hence the backaches.

I had not given much thought to miscarrying a baby. I had always been healthy and strong, and my first pregnancy had gone so well, except for the difficult birth. Miscarriages happened to other people, not me. I scheduled the procedure that needed to be done and went home in a daze. I was confused and I think in denial until, before my appointment with the doctor, I miscarried at home. Then the realization began to hit home. I would not be having my baby girl in September. My instinct for self-preservation told me that it was for the best. Something wasn't right and the pregnancy was not to be. I had my little Ryan, and life would go on.

The next day I went to my appointment, after being told I still needed the procedure, and met with my doctor in his office afterwards. I had remained rational and thought I was going to get through this loss without too much pain until he sat down, took my hand, and looked into my eyes. My world collapsed at that moment. Suddenly I knew that I had lost my daughter, or son. That little person had been a very real part of my life, and now, for whatever unexplained reason, it had been taken from me. I cried and cried while Dr. Newton held me, understanding that my pain was very real. When I regained my composure, he consoled me, and assured me that there was no reason why I could not have as many healthy babies as I wanted, and that I could start trying again after six months. I did recover and soon got back to my busy life, but I never forgot that experience, wondering from time to time if that was to have been my daughter, and if I had unknowingly done something to cause the miscarriage. I don't beat myself up over it, I just wonder.

~

1985 brought another unwelcome turn of events. Still working, I relished the opportunity to see the entire state in all seasons, and to get breaks, overnighting in warm cities in the Lower 48. Mark continued to struggle taking care of Ryan while I was away, but he had learned to manage his time more efficiently, and a toddler is easier to care for than an infant, but it put a strain on him. I felt guilty leaving them, but neither of us considered giving up the great pay, travel benefits, and flexible schedule I enjoyed at Wien, when suddenly, out of the blue, Wien Air Alaska announced they would be ceasing operations. Ceasing operations? After Sixty years of service in Alaska? Wien was a symbol of Alaska. Everyone flew on the Wieney bird. Wien connected us as Alaskans, to each other, and to the adventures otherwise out of our reach. The entire state was abuzz with the news.

Apparently, the plan to sell Wien's assets to Alaska Airlines and a small local airline had been in the works for sometime. Other crew members and I remembered seeing an Alaska Airlines jet at the Phoenix airport and wondered why it was there, since they did not serve Phoenix. Now we understood they were setting up their operations to be ready for when Wien left. Realizing that the signs had been there did not lessen the shock.

It was the end of an era, an era of daring bush pilots, jets landing on gravel airstrips at remote villages, and a group of employees that embodied the true Alaskan spirit. Many of the exceptional pilots who neared the end of their careers with Wien found themselves without the retirement they had counted on, and too old to find work with other airlines. They were truly victims of this "business transaction." All of us employees who had faced the extreme weather, the mechanical failures, the medical transports, and some of the most unique, once-in-a-lifetime experiences together, went into mourning. In mourning for the end of this historic airline that had become so much a part of each of us.

Even though it has been thirty years since the end of Wien, the ex-employees still have reunions and keep in touch. For me, it marked a special time and place that enriched my life more than any other. I would not trade those years for anything.

Before Wien's last flight, I was contacted by Alaska Airlines and offered a job as a flight attendant with them. My hopes soared as I thought maybe I could continue my career. Unfortunately, Alaska Airlines would not be maintaining a crew base in Anchorage, and I would have been based in Seattle. That was not a major issue for my childless co-workers. Many flight crews do not live in their base city, commuting (deadheading) on flights to and from their home town. But for me it meant more time away from my family, and I was not willing to make that sacrifice. We decided I would stay home with Ryan and continue to help with our businesses on my own schedule. It really was the right decision for us, and a huge load off Mark's shoulders. He was once again free to work around the clock, which the midnight sun allowed him to do. Most of the time I was too busy to miss my old job, but sometimes I longed to be jetting off to some isolated village or pipeline camp high in the icy Brooks Mountain Range, or to a mini warm-weather break in Phoenix. Those adventures were over for me, but I will always cherish the memories.

My eight year adventure as a
Wien Air Alaska flight attendant comes to an end.

ALASKA AIRBOAT TOURS

If there is one thing I don't have to worry about while being married to Mark, it's getting bored. I never know what he is going to do next. He has more energy than any one person should be allowed to have. And he is always on the lookout for ways to make money. Sometimes, though, I do have to rein him in, as he can be led down the wrong path, if there is supposed to be money at the end of it. This was the case when he came home telling me about a business he was thinking about starting with an associate of his. "We would be taking tourists up Knik River to the Knik Glacier on air boats like they use in the Everglades."

"What?" I asked "We don't know anything about air boats."

"There will be three of us, the boat mechanic, the salesman, and me, the financier," he explained. "We are going up to the river this Sunday to see the boats in action."

Well, I just couldn't imagine how this was going to work out, but I kept an open mind, and Sunday morning we went to meet Hal, the first partner. Hal would be the salesman for the business, and this meeting was my first sign that this venture was not going to work. To me it was obvious that Hal was a big blowhard, but Mark is a poor judge of people, and he was convinced that Hal would be a great partner. He had worked with him on construction projects, and knew him to be successful. I was thinking that you had to be really incompetent to not have experienced some success during the pipeline boom in Alaska, but at this point, I kept my doubts to myself.

The three of us drove out to the river to meet Leonard, the third partner, and take a ride up to the Knik Glacier. Leonard was the builder, mechanic, and operator of the boats. His job would be to drive the boats and keep them maintained and in good working order. As soon as we were introduced, warning flag number two went up. At this point my woman's intuition told me Leonard was not business partner material, even though I knew very little about him. However, as women know, our intuition is a powerful resource, and not to be disregarded. Leonard had all three of his boats in the water and ready to go.

Large, flat-bottomed, with automobile engines and airplane propellers on the back, this type of boat is used on Alaskan rivers traditional boats cannot navigate because of the shallow areas. Noise poses one serious problem with these boats. That is an airplane propeller roaring behind you as you make your way to the glacier. Not a very pleasant tourist experience, if you ask me. But wait, Leonard had protective ear guards, for everyone to wear, the same type used by airport ground crews. Okay, I donned the ear guards and got onboard one of the boats, reminding myself to keep an open mind.

To make a long story short, none of the boats were capable of making it to the glacier that day. In fact, none of them could even leave the shore. Leonard had one excuse after another relating to the operation of the boats. At this point I knew this whole "Airboat Tours" idea was a bad one. Despite all the warning signs, Mark, Hal, and Leonard insisted they could make it work. I strongly voiced my opinion, but was criticized for being a negative person and not supportive of their exciting new venture, and they went forward with their plans.

Within a few months they had the operation up and running, and did actually get some tourists up to the glacier. The problem was that it was so expensive keeping the boats running, and Mark was "investing" so much money, that it eventually became clear to him making a profit would be nearly impossible. After that first year of operation, and a large sum of money, Mark decided to call it quits. At this point in our young lives, Mark had not learned to listen when I offered advice about a business venture. He did eventually learn, but not before several expensive, ill-advised investments.

Today there is a company offering this same tour on the Knik River, so I must admit, it was a workable idea. Mark says he was just ahead of the times.

Alaska Airboat Tours

A GIRL'S BEST FRIEND
(And a Guy's Too)

One of the businesses that opened in Anchorage to take advantage of the prosperous economy was the large and glittery Gold and Diamond Company. Haines Construction, Inc. had built the fancy new building, and we were invited to the grand opening. The young wheeler-dealer owner stocked the store with jewels and gems from around the world. At the grand opening event, our eyes sparkled, reflecting the light from the lit showcases filled with rubies, emeralds, sapphires, and of course diamonds.

Christmas neared, and Pat, who made very good money as Haines Construction's lead foreman, decided he would buy his wife a gift of diamonds. Not to be outdone by his employee, Mark bought me a beautiful diamond to replace my less-impressive wedding ring. And so started the year of the diamonds. Upon hearing about the gifts Mark and Pat would be presenting their wives come Christmas morning, all the husbands in our group figured they better get something sparkly for their wives, too. After Christmas, we all showed off our beautiful gifts and our husbands were our heroes.

At some point during this time of plenty, I decided that Mark should have a nice ring, too. He had a gold wedding band, which he had rarely worn because he worked in construction, but I thought he deserved a diamond ring to wear when we went out and when we traveled. One Sunday morning, while having coffee and reading the newspaper, I spotted an ad for a new jewelry store opening soon. The ad included a credit application, which, once submitted, entered you in a contest for a $5,000 store credit. The winner would be announced when they opened a few weeks later. I grabbed a pen and filled out the application in Mark's name and sent it in.

A few weeks later, while enjoying my Sunday morning routine of coffee and the newspaper, I saw that the new store was opening that day, and the winner of the contest would be announced, but had to be present to win. The drawing would be at noon, and I noticed it was 11:30. Should we go, I wondered? I never win anything; Mark, however does win. I called the store to find out how many people were there, and the clerk said not too many, and our chances were pretty good. I decided it was worth a drive into town. I rustled up Mark and two-year-old Ryan, and away we went.

The clerk had been right; there were not very many people there. The owner prepared for the drawing, putting all the names of the applicants on little pieces of ribbon and putting them in a large fish bowl. We admired the cases, filled mostly with emeralds, until the owner noticed Mark wandering around the store holding Ryan in his arms, and asked if he could borrow Ryan to draw the winning name out of the bowl. "Sure," Mark said. "He will think it's a game." They announced the drawing, and everyone gathered around in hopes of winning the prize. The owner lifted the bowl to Ryan, still in Mark's arms, and asked him to pick one ribbon out of the bowl. Ryan reached in, pulled out a ribbon, and handed it to the owner, who read the name out loud. There was no response, and it was soon determined that since you had to be present to win, another ribbon would have to be drawn. Once again, Ryan reached his little hand into the bowl and presented a ribbon to the owner.

"Mark Haines," he read. "Is Mark Haines here?" Oh my gosh, I thought. Mark won! Everyone was looking around them to see if Mark Haines were there, as Mark told the owner that it was him.

"You're Mark Haines? And this is your son?" The news quickly spread throughout the small crowd, and a few grumbles that it was a little suspicious that the winner's son had drawn the name. The owner and his manager disappeared into a back room while I held my breath, hoping they weren't going to disqualify us. *Ryan was only two for goodness sake. It is not as if he could read the names on the ribbons.* After a couple of minutes, the owner came back out front and announced that Mark Haines was indeed the winner of the $5,000 store credit, and since his little boy drew his dad's name, he was adding another $1,500 to his prize, all to be redeemed at a special dinner a few weeks' from then. He would let us know the exact date later.

I was so excited! A $6,500 credit in a jewelry store! And the fact that our little boy had drawn his dad's name made winning even more special. Every weekend I wanted to go to the jewelry store, (I can't remember the name after all these years) and see what new items had come in and decide what we wanted to choose. Mark was always too busy and not really interested to go shopping, and figured we would go when they called to let us know it was time for the presentation. In my opinion, too much time went by, and one

Saturday I insisted we go down and find out when we could claim our winnings.

When we pulled into the parking lot, I wondered why there were no cars parked out front. Were they closed on a Saturday afternoon? As we walked up to the entry, to our dismay, the store was empty! No showcases filled with jewelry, no salesmen and no customers. “What happened?” I asked. “Have they moved?”

Mark read a notice posted on the window. “Apparently this store was a front for a Columbian cocaine smuggling ring. They have been busted, and all their assets have been seized by the authorities,” he explained.

“But what about our credit?” I questioned.

“I doubt there was ever going to be a credit,” he replied. “It was probably all just a big show.”

“But we won the contest.” I protested. “We are owed our winnings.”

“Get in line,” Mark said, “They probably owe everybody involved with this company. There will be no prize for us.”

I was crestfallen. Mark was more upset about the fact that we couldn’t tell the story that Ryan had drawn his dad’s name out of the fish bowl, winning him a beautiful ring. As we stood in the parking lot, deflated and forlorn, we looked up and saw the sign for the Gold and Diamond Company across the street. “I’m going to go see George,” Mark said. “I may just buy myself a diamond ring.” I guessed he was more disappointed than I thought.

I wasn’t so sure he would actually buy himself a diamond ring, but after telling Pat, his foreman, the story of the cocaine dealers, they went together to look at rings. Mark came home with a beautiful two-carat solitaire diamond ring. The stone was stunning, and perfect for him, it fit on his strong, masculine hand just right. Not to be outdone, Pat bought himself a beautiful fancy brown diamond, also set in yellow gold. It was out of character for these guys to be buying themselves expensive jewelry, but as I mentioned, George, the owner, was a wheeler-dealer, and was always ready to accommodate his clients, and the boys seemed to had caught "diamond fever."

You might think the diamond story ends here, but, as fate would have it, it continued. One evening, after a night out on the town, Mark was washing up before bed, and upon trying to remove the ring from his slightly swollen finger, it went flying off, ricocheting off the sides of the porcelain sink, finally coming to rest near the drain. He retrieved it and was shocked to discover the stone had a monumental crack right through the center. "My ring!" he exclaimed. "I have broken the stone!"

"What do you mean you've broken the stone? How do you break a diamond?" I asked. I didn't know you could break a diamond, but we learned that night that if it hits a hard surface just right, it will definitely break. The crack went from the surface, through the center of the stone, all the way to the tip at the bottom, totally ruining it. We were sick about it. Luckily, we had purchased insurance for our jewelry and called the agent first thing Monday morning. The ring was covered, and we would receive a check for the market value. Next Mark called George, our jewelry connection at the Gold and Diamond Company, and told him we needed to replace the stone we had purchased from him.

A few days later, George called Mark telling him he had a couple of options for him to consider. We could replace the stone with a similar one, or he had a larger stone that he wanted Mark to see. The larger stone was a hair under three carats. Apparently the cutter had made a huge mistake, cutting just a little too much off of the stone bringing the weight to just under three carats, causing the value of the stone to decrease dramatically. It was also in the yellow range, not yellow enough to be considered fancy, but close. This also contributed to the value of this larger stone being close to the value of the two-carat. When we saw the stone, we knew immediately we - notice I say we - wanted the larger stone. Not only was it really big, it glowed like a harvest moon.

George set the stone in the yellow-gold setting, which enhanced its mesmerizing glow, and Mark still wears it today. I often picture it around my neck as a necklace, but at least I get to admire it when he wears it. His mother caught diamond fever, too, when she came to Anchorage on a visit. She felt left out, admiring our beautiful diamond rings. Mark took her down to shop at George's store, and she came home with a stunner. A ring that I admired on her Mediterranean skin every time I saw her wear it. The secondary, baguette-cut stones, merged together with the center diamond, artistically, to create a bold and at the same time delicate look. I have since inherited that ring, and I wear it frequently. It reminds me of her, and of our shared love of jewelry. And of that unique time of plenty in our beloved Alaska.

~

For the first time in my adult life, I did not have a job of my own. I continued to help Mark with his business, running errands, paying bills, and of course taking care of Ryan and our lovely home, but still, something seemed to be missing. I had become a travel agent after leaving Wien, but I did not want to work full time, and Mark was, by now, dependent on me. While pondering what I would do next, I learned I was pregnant again. *So this is what I'm going to do next*, I thought: *Have another baby.*

Chapter 7

BUST

All good things come to an end. And the end of the boom times in Alaska came suddenly, with little warning, plunging the state into financial decline. The energy crisis of the 1970s had driven the price of oil to $40 a barrel in 1981. The world's thirst for oil had fueled Alaska's pipeline boom, and while the price of oil remained high, money flowed into the state, making up about one-third of its economic base. When the price of oil plummeted to less than $15 a barrel in March of 1986, the impact devastated Alaska. The population was blindsided. Most of us were there specifically to work and make money. What will happen, we wondered? Soon, as we learned from our local news stations, it would no longer be profitable for the oil companies to drill for and sell Alaska's oil. The handwriting on the wall became frighteningly clear.

The dominoes started falling immediately as the oil companies slowed production, laying off workers, and sending them back to their homes in the Lower 48. The large number of oil company employees leaving created a ripple effect, as rental units emptied out and businesses suffered the loss of those customers. The robust construction business came to a screeching halt, sending all the carpenters and laborers south, as they could no longer afford the high cost of living in Alaska. For the first time in seven years, Haines Construction, Inc., had no projects waiting to be built.

The impact of this unexpected economic downturn devastated the two of us. We had always done so well financially, always growing our businesses and making lots of money with both of us working, our rental income, and our extremely profitable construction company. Now I was pregnant, and bringing in no money, Haines Construction, Inc., was dead in the water, and the panic really began to set in as our tenants began vacating our apartment units, one right after another. These apartment buildings had large mortgages to be paid every month, and even though we had a solid savings account, we had not planned for a financial crisis this extreme.

Our lives changed so fast. Another loss met us every day. Ryan's preschool closed and we had to say goodbye to his favorite teacher and classmates, and our favorite restaurant closed its doors, too. Half of the homes in Anchorage went up for sale, as the owners had lost their jobs and had no way to pay the mortgage. People began defaulting on their home mortgages, needing to relocate somewhere they could find work. Our friends and acquaintances, and the lives we had lived and loved for the last twelve years, quickly disappeared. As much as we wanted to preserve our picture perfect-world, Anchorage was no longer the exciting boom town we had known, and it pained us to see those times end. We knew that some tough decisions needed to be made.

~

Neither one of us wanted to leave. Anchorage had become our home. I planned to have our second child there, and bring him or her home to the house we had built together. Mark wanted to keep his company going and continue the adventure of being challenged by the environment. We both loved the beauty that surrounded us and the novelty of living in the last frontier. But if we stayed, would we be able to weather the storm?

On the other-hand, it was never going to be the same. Almost everyone we knew was leaving. Our once thriving city now sadly declined. I had begun regretting being so far from our families, especially now that we were having another child. Maybe it was time to leave, we just didn't know. I did know that I wanted to stay put until the baby was born, at the very least. We also had to figure out what to do with our vacant apartment buildings, the construction company, and all of our other commitments.

~

Being baby boomers, Mark and I were raised believing that when you make a promise, you do everything in your power to keep it. Mark had been wrestling with getting tenants in our empty units to help cover costs. We had been making the monthly payments on these properties for months now, and our savings accounts dwindled fast. He managed to get a smattering of tenants, which helped, but in no way covered the mortgages. We had heard that the banks were working with borrowers, reducing interest rates, or taking reduced payments. We decided it was time to sit down with our mortgage holders and see what could be worked out. To our dismay, the bankers flatly refused to take anything but full payment on our loans. They had looked over our finances and decided we were rich enough to meet the original terms of the loans. Mark pointed out that the financials they were looking at were several years old, and, as they were well aware, things had changed drastically. He offered to have all rents go directly to the bank, or make a reduced payment, or meet any new terms they saw fit. No, no, they didn't want to hear any of that. Pay the full amount and that was that.

We were beside ourselves, not knowing what to do about these debts. Everyone told us to just turn the keys over to them. "Why continue to throw money at a losing proposition. That is what everyone else has done," they told us. "All the people who have left, handed their property back to the bank." We considered what we were being told and realized that we were the only people we knew who were still making payments on their distressed properties. For us, it was not an easy decision.

After several more failed attempts to reason with the bankers, we agreed it was foolish to continue paying on the apartment buildings until we depleted our reserves. We would need that money to start over if we decided to move. We figured we would have to default on the buildings when the money ran out, anyway, so we might as well do it while we still had something left. Mark gathered all the keys and the few rental agreements we had and went to turn them over to the bank.

"Nope, no, we don't want that property back," the banker told Mark. "We have more worthless property than we should have ever taken back, and we are not taking yours. If you quit making the payments, we will sue you for the balance of the loans."

We didn't realize they could do that, but that is exactly what they did. Now we had a lawsuit to fight, in addition to our mounting bills, and no income. We tried to keep a normal routine around the house for Ryan and me, as my pregnancy progressed. At dinner one night, Paul and Patti told us that Patti was being transferred soon, and they had to choose between relocating to Los Angeles, California, or Portland, Oregon. This was another blow to us, as they had been our closest friends, and we considered them our

Alaskan family. Mark had been putting feelers out within the construction community, gathering information about where companies were moving, but in the back of our minds, we assumed we would return to California if we left. With that in mind, Mark registered to start the California contractors licensing process, meaning he would be traveling to Sacramento to attend the courses, while Ryan and I stayed at home.

~

Mark was gone for weeks at a time that winter, and Ryan and I settled into a comfortable routine. I found a daycare for Ryan while I took care of what remained of our businesses, and went to my exercise class as I had done during my first pregnancy. At one of my doctor's visits, the nurse commented that my blood pressure was on the high side and I should check it regularly. On the way home from my exercise class the next day, I stopped at our neighborhood clinic and asked them to check my blood pressure. By this time, I was about seven months pregnant, and not feeling as chipper as I had while I carried Ryan.

"Your blood pressure is dangerously high!" the nurse exclaimed. "We need to get you to the hospital immediately," she told me, as she rushed off to get the doctor.

I didn't feel any different, and could only assure myself that the nurse was over-reacting. However, when the doctor came in frowning, asking lots of questions, and telling the nurse to notify the hospital that I would be coming in, I got a little anxious, but not overly so.

Later I found myself in a hospital bed with an IV in my arm, wondering what happened. I hadn't talked to a doctor and only knew that my blood pressure was high. I began to worry about Ryan. He was safe at the daycare, but he would have to be picked up before 6:00 p.m. I noticed it was only 2:00 p.m., and assumed I would be released well before 6:00 p.m. I tried to relax, wishing Mark were in town to be with me.

Later, when the nurse came back in, I asked if I would be released soon, and she replied, "You're not going anywhere with your blood pressure this high. Just relax and the doctor will see you soon."

By now it was getting late in the afternoon, and I was anxious about getting Ryan picked up. I had to call someone. I knew Patti was still at work, but I hoped I would be able to reach Paul. Luckily he answered my call and said he would get Ryan, and then come down to the hospital. He assured me they would keep Ryan as long as needed, and that I need not worry. Grateful for his reassurance, I did relax momentarily. When the doctor finally made his appearance, my numbers were normalizing, and he expected I would be able to leave the hospital within the hour, however….

"You have a mild case of toxemia, and you will have to stay in bed and be monitored more closely until the baby is born."

"Stay in bed? But I have six weeks to go!" I exclaimed, while the realization that I had a three-year-old to care for, and no help, started to sink in. "All day? All the time? How will I manage?" I asked.

"You must find a way. If you are up more than two hours a day, you and your baby will be at risk. I will go sign you out. You can leave when the nurse comes in with the papers." I stared at the door as it closed behind him and the questions started forming in my mind. Can I drive? What is toxemia, and why do I have it? How soon will Mark be able to get back home? While I pondered these questions Paul arrived with Ryan. I was so happy to see them and just wanted to go home.

The nurse answered my immediate questions, explaining that the baby can't get the food and oxygen it needs if I don't keep my blood pressure down. I could drive and stay up the allowed two hours, but I should stay in bed the rest of the time. I thanked Paul, telling him I would call if I needed anything, and drove home. Once we were fed and in bed with a movie on for Ryan, I called Mark, with the hope he would rush right home.

Men are so different from women. If I ever received a call from Mark telling me he needed me, I would drop whatever I was doing and come to his side. I guess that is because women are typically the caregivers. Men, on the other hand, are wired to be the provider, and providing for our family was Mark's number one priority. Of course he was concerned about us, but was right in the middle of his course, and did not want to waste the weeks he had already put into it. "He can stay at the daycare all day, and you have two hours to care for him before bed in the evenings. You can watch movies and read to him; he will love that," he reasoned. "I only have a couple more weeks, and then I will be home."

"I guess we can try it." I answered. But after we hung up, I started thinking of all I would have to get done in those two hours: Getting Ryan to and from his daycare, getting my blood pressure checked, shopping, preparing meals, bathing us both, and any other chores and errands that might come up. Well, I thought, I will just have to be very efficient.

I managed to get it all done and get the two of us settled in bed to watch a video or two, and then read stories until Ryan went to sleep. I know I went over the two hours a few times, but my blood pressure stayed where it needed to be. Ryan was happy as a clam. We normally restricted his television time, and to be able to watch movies every night was a treat for him. We did fine, and soon it was time for Mark to come home. It was a huge relief for me having him home, but he had a hard time understanding that his girl Friday had to stay in bed. So used to me always being available for whatever he needed me to do, he couldn't grasp the seriousness of my condition.

We still did not know if we were going to leave the state, or try to outlast the bad times. We truly loved Alaska, and I think Mark would have stayed forever despite the lack of work, but I missed my family and leaned towards leaving. With that in mind, we decided to put the house up for sale just to see what would happen. With so many properties on the market, we really didn't think there would be any response. At the same time, since Mark's business remained slow, he started having garage sales, cleaning out closets and getting rid of accumulated "stuff " in preparation for a possible move.

~

One afternoon we had a meeting with our financial advisors. I saved my two hours because I needed to be at the meeting. The baby was due in two weeks, and I was getting pretty uncomfortable. It was good to be out in the world, and I stayed up a little longer than I should have, and by the time we got home, I was really tired and achy, and feeling kind of strange. I stayed downstairs, partially reclining on the floor, and playing with Ryan for a while - but just did not feel well, so I went up to bed, hoping to get some sleep.

There was no comfortable position for my swollen body, and I tossed and turned and just couldn't relax. Then I began to suspect that my discomfort was due to the onset of labor. I wondered if I had overdone it, staying up so long, causing labor to start early. Sure enough, the pains began around midnight. They were not bad at first, and I decided I would stay home longer this time since my water hadn't broken, and go to the hospital in the morning. Our plan was for Paul and Patti to watch Ryan while we were at the hospital, but we did not expect to need them this early, and they were in Portland, Oregon, looking at houses. What will we do with him? I wondered. I feared I might be in for another thirty-six-hour labor.

My labor pains gradually progressed through the night, but we waited until a decent hour to start calling people who might be able to watch Ryan. Everyone we called was unavailable on such short notice, and finally we called Patti's sister, our last resort. She already had Nathan, Paul and Patti's son, and was a little hesitant, not having any children still at home, so she worried about managing two active little boys. I explained our predicament, and she agreed to take him. Now that we were sure Ryan would be occupied playing with an older friend that he looked up to, we headed to the hospital.

I don't know why I choose the weekend to go into labor, but my doctor was once again out of town. I had never met the doctor on-call who checked on my progress, determining I had a long way to go. "Great," I thought, discouraged. "This is going to take forever. I don't know if I can do it again. I want to go home." Of course that was out of the question, and the doctor decided he was going to go to the shooting range in Eagle River and do some target practice.

Feeling even more discouraged, I asked, "You're leaving? Isn't Eagle River kind of far?

"I don't think anything will happen for a while, and I have my pager and can be back here in twenty minutes," he replied.

I decided it didn't matter. I could lay here and suffer without him. It appeared we were the only ones in the maternity ward, and once the doctor had gone, it was just us and our nurse. Mark feared a long ordeal also, and said: "I am going down to the cafeteria to get something to eat before your pains get bad." Actually they were already pretty bad, but what did he know about it? "I'll be back in a while." And he disappeared down the hall.

The nurse had been gone a while, and I lay there by myself staring at the ceiling and monitoring my contractions, when suddenly, I was gripped with a serious cramp. *Oh no*, I thought. *I am going to have diarrhea! This is serious. I have to get to the bathroom.* I scooted off the bed, supporting myself as I made my way to the bathroom, and finally managed to situate myself on the toilet just as another pain gripped my stomach - the urge to eliminate was overwhelming. Then it dawned on me, "This is not diarrhea, I am in transition. I have to get up before I have this baby right here in the toilet."

I got up and grabbed the door frame, by now sweating and panting with pain, and managed to get back on the bed. *I have to get the nurse. Where is the buzzer?* Then I remembered it was on the wall, and for some unknown reason, the bed had been pulled away from the wall. Try as I might, I couldn't reach the call button. "Help, someone, I need help," I screamed. *Where is that nurse? Am I going to have this baby all by myself!* I wondered

She finally burst into the room. "What's wrong?"

"I think the baby is coming. I feel like I can push him out right now!"

"Don't push, don't push yet. Let me have a look." She quickly checked and exclaimed: "You're right, the baby is ready to be born, but don't push, let me find a doctor." And she rushed out.

Don't push, I thought. *They better hurry, because I can't not push for much longer.*

I assume she paged my doctor at target practice, but realizing he was at least twenty minutes away went to find the resident on duty, who happened to be the only doctor in the hospital at that moment. When they arrived back at my room, Mark had returned and was in a panic, and I moaned and cried that I needed to push. The poor resident stood in the doorway watching, too petrified to even come in. His body language said: *I have never delivered a baby; I want no part of this.*

The nurse told me not to push, the doctor was on his way, if I could just wait a few more minutes. *Are these people crazy?* I thought. *When a baby wants to come you can't just stop it.* I soon discovered that you can stop it, and stop it I did. When the doctor finally made his appearance, and announced I could now push, the labor pains had completely stopped, and there was no way the baby was coming. He kept telling me to push, and I assured him my pushing was a waste of time because nothing was happening. He had several other great ideas, including having me hang from a sort of trapeze that was rigged up above my bed. Apparently hanging from a trapeze is supposed to get the baby to come out. Then he decided to try to push the baby out from the outside of my stomach - again, nothing.

By now I was getting really frustrated, knowing that the baby wouldn't be born because I was hanging from a bar, or because the doctor pushed on my stomach. After a few hours of being hung up, pushed on, and in my opinion, abused, I once again began to feel the labor pains. "Hang from this bar again," the doctor advised. I sighed, not seeing the benefit of hanging from a bar. Just then, the nurse whispered in my ear: "Turn over on your left side." Within minutes, the pains went to maximum force and I began to push, and the startled doctor stepped into place to catch baby Aaron as he quickly and easily made his appearance. Why the doctor didn't suggest turning on my side I don't know, but I am so grateful that the nurse was there to coach me.

As soon as I held my new son, all the pain and frustration vanished, and I once again knew the intense love that only a mother can feel for her child. He was so different from my overdue, plump and alert Ryan, being early, tiny and weak, but I instantly loved him, unconditionally.

Me with my baby, Aaron

~

Marks's mother and stepdad arrived that day, having tried to be there for the birth, but not quite making it. They were enchanted with their new grandson and we all returned home with our bundle of joy. Knowing that I could be up and around, despite just giving birth, made me feel as if I had a lot of energy. To keep our guests entertained we continued with the garage sale, finding more and more items we could live without and moving them out to the garage which was opened each day for shoppers. It felt good to be getting rid of clutter and items we knew we would not need in the Lower 48, especially as it seemed we would eventually be leaving. There had been no response to our "For Sale" sign until a Japan Airlines pilot showed up at our door one afternoon, wanting to lease the house.

We agonized over the decision to leave so suddenly, but decided we could not turn down the opportunity to have the house leased at a good price for two years. The movers came, we packed up, and the kids and I headed to my parents' house, leaving Mark behind to tie up loose ends.

Chapter 8

STARTING OVER

It wasn't easy staying at my parents. Ryan was confused and missed his dad, and I felt like a gypsy, with no home of my own and no husband around. My parents were wonderful, enjoying their grandkids and pampering me, and I reconnected with my old friends who had also become mothers. Even so, I longed to be settled somewhere with my little family.

While still up in Anchorage, Mark was persuaded to partner with a contractor friend of his in Phoenix, Arizona. He finished up in Alaska, came to stay with us for a short time, and then left for Phoenix to get licensed over there, once again leaving us behind. I was not on board with the Phoenix plan, I could not see us being successful there. Mark, however, was convinced this was the place to go. After four months at my parents', we packed up and moved to Phoenix. We found a nice house to rent, had all of our furniture moved from storage in Seattle, and settled in. I hated it from the moment we arrived.

I just could not adjust to Arizona. Mark was consumed with getting his business started, but I was home with a four-year-old and an infant. I did not know a soul, couldn't find my way around, hated the heat, and felt lonely and out of place. To make matters worse, Mark was not having any luck getting jobs, and finances were tight. Baby Aaron didn't like it either. He cried all night for about six weeks, and I thought I would go crazy. One afternoon I loaded the boys up in the car and headed to the mall for some retail therapy. I thought I knew where I was going, but I drove and drove until I realized I had no idea where I was. Both of the boys had fallen asleep in the back seat, and I pulled the car off the road and sat there and cried, feeling lost, lonely, and depressed. I turned the car around and went back home.

Mark came home that evening announcing that he had a job in San Diego and would be going there to work. It was a small job, and he wouldn't be gone long. Well, a job is a job, I thought, maybe this is the beginning for his new company. It turned out to be the first of many jobs, but the problem was they were all in San Diego! He was over there all the time and the kids and I were stuck in Phoenix. This was not the way it was supposed to be, and I made my feelings known.

The construction industry was booming in southern California, and Mark saw that it was time to make another change. Nothing was happening construction-wise in Phoenix, so he finally agreed that San Diego was a much better option for us. We decided to make the move and drove over to look for a house to rent and feel the place out. The real estate market was going crazy that year, so we decided we should buy instead of rent. The agent showing us rentals told us it would be very hard to purchase a house in a tight market like this, but he knew of a one-year-old house that was not selling due to some aesthetic issues. When we went to see it, we discovered what those issues were. The interior of the house was red. Red everything, red wallpaper, red window coverings - and I don't mean a little red, I mean a lot of red. The bright red was turning buyers off, but we knew it was a matter of redecorating, and then it would be a great house in a great neighborhood. We made an offer on the house, which was accepted, and headed back home, leaving Kraig, our agent, to arrange financing.

~

Once we were back in Phoenix, Mark immediately turned around and went back to San Diego. He had another job, and more lined up after that. Things were looking up, and I set about packing us up for our move back to California. I couldn't wait to get out of Phoenix. Nine months was nine months too long, as far as I was concerned. I am not sure why I had such a negative experience in Arizona. I had loved it when I had layovers there, enjoying the warm climate and the scent of orange blossoms. Mark and I had taken a couple of short winter breaks to Phoenix from Alaska and had enjoyed our time there also. I guess it was because it was a difficult time for me. Having to leave our home in Anchorage, not knowing anyone in this new neighborhood, and dealing with a case of postpartum depression. Now, I was feeling new life, knowing in my heart we were doing the right thing.

While Mark was in San Diego, he finalized our loan on our new house - no small feat considering we had not settled the lawsuit over the apartments in Anchorage - and let me know he would be returning soon. All of our belongings were packed and ready; I had hired the movers, and was caring for Ryan, who had caught a bad case of chicken pox from a neighbor. The poor kid was a mess. I could tell how bad he felt as he lay in bed covered with red, itchy blisters. I assumed he would be well in time for our drive to California. Mark had returned to get us, and the movers were scheduled to be there the next morning, when I noticed those little chicken-pox blisters breaking out on one-year-old Aaron.

Luckily Aaron had a mild case of chicken pox, and we were able to stick to our plan. After the movers left, we loaded our vehicles with what we would need for two days and hit the road, Ryan in the truck with Mark, and sick little Aaron with me. I was ecstatic to be leaving. The sun was setting over the desert and on our time there, and I never looked back. We stopped at a hotel about halfway, dealing with a fussy baby who was getting tired of being jostled all around while he didn't feel well. When we arrived in San

Diego, the house was not ready for us, so Mark arranged for us to stay with one of his employees for the night. We were already worn out, having had a rough night at the hotel the night before with Aaron not fully recovered, so when Ryan woke me up soon after we had retired, struggling with an asthma attack, I resigned myself to another sleepless night. He was allergic to cats, and even though they had removed their cats from the house, he still got sick. We had to get him out of there. We packed up and headed out into the night to find a hotel. I had his inhalers, and he soon breathed normally. Resettled at a freeway side motel, we hoped to get a few hours' rest.

Mark had a big job starting the next day in Los Angeles, so we got up early and headed to our new home. He dropped us off to meet the movers, who were already arriving, and off he went for the rest of the week. Thankfully both of the boys had slept once we finally got them to bed, and Aaron seemed to be recovering from the chicken pox. They were interested in all the activity, but were understandably clingy. Our friendly new neighbors came over to welcome us and offer much appreciated assistance, and I set about directing the movers who maneuvered around the painters and carpet cleaners, who were still finishing up.

With Aaron balanced on one hip and Ryan by my side, I continued directing the placement of our belongings, paid the carpet cleaners, inspected the painter's touch-up job, and thought I handled the chaos pretty well. Then the doorbell rang, and I remembered I had scheduled the cable and telephone installation, and wouldn't you know it, they both arrived at the same time!

"Where do you want the cable outlets, lady?

"I can get started on the phone lines as soon as you show me where you want your phones. How many outlets do you want?"

"Where do you want this dresser, it's really heavy?"

"Hold on," I exclaimed, setting Aaron down, and asking Ryan to sit on the stairs with him and hold his hand. A few minutes later, as I rushed back and forth between the workers and installers,

I felt Ryan tugging on my pant leg. "I am very busy right now honey, what is it?" I asked.

"Aaron has diarrhea, you better come," he said, with eyes as big as saucers.

I rushed into the entry way and found Aaron standing there crying. Yes, he had diarrhea, and it was leaking out of his diaper, and running down his legs. He looked so pitiful I felt as if I had been neglecting him, and Ryan, too, but there was only one of me. Aaron was just getting over the chicken pox, and I should have been more attentive to him. I felt awful and sat down on the stairs with my face in my hands trying to hold back the tears. Just then the moving men came through the door with our king-sized mattress, and I looked at them through my fingers and asked them to put the mattress down right where they were; I would be with them in a few minutes. They seemed to sense that I had reached my limit and set the mattress down without saying anything. The cable and phone guys suddenly quieted, also. I grabbed my diaper bag and took Ryan and Aaron upstairs for some privacy and cleaned Aaron up. Then we sat on the floor, and I hugged and rocked them while I regained my composure. *I have to get through this day.* I told myself. That few minutes of quiet with my boys, who seemed fine, grounded me for the rest of the afternoon.

Finally, everyone was gone except the moving men, who had the truck emptied and were getting ready to go. It was getting late, and I knew I still had beds to put together and linens to unpack, and having given the boys the last of the snacks I had with me, wondered what we would eat for dinner. Somehow I persuaded the movers to put our beds together, which is not in their job description, while the boys and I ran out to get fast food. When we returned with our hamburgers, we thanked the movers for their excellent work and waved to them as they drove off, leaving us alone for the first time that day. We ate our dinner and proceeded to open the boxes marked "Linens," finding our sheets, pillows, and blankets. Once the beds were made, I gave the boys a warm bath, sat in the rocking chair, with Ryan resting on a pillow on the floor beside us, while I fed Aaron his bottle. He was soon sound asleep. Once Ryan was tucked in his bed I read him a short story, and he drifted off before I finished. We were all exhausted.

The house seemed so big, quiet, and a little spooky. I didn't know anything about this neighborhood and was a little uneasy. It was only 8:30 p.m., but I was ready to lock up and get ready for bed. I locked all the windows and the back doors, then stepped out the front door to catch the last of the lovely June sunset. I took a couple of deep breaths and began to feel we had found our home, so I headed back inside to lock the door behind me.

I couldn't get the door to lock. Try as I might, it just wouldn't lock. In fact, it wouldn't even stay closed. The slightest wind blew the door open! *What am I going to do?* I wondered. *I can't go to bed with the door wide open. I could put a chair in front of it, but that doesn't seem very safe. I have my babies upstairs and I have no idea if this neighborhood is safe.* Then I remembered my friendly neighbors. They said if I needed anything not to hesitate to ask, so I ran next door, hoping they meant it.

They were nothing but kindness. The dad and teenage son came right over, checked the door, ran back home to grab some tools, and soon the door was in perfect working order. Finally, this hectic day was over. I trudged upstairs to get some rest. My parents were driving down from the Bay Area the next day to help me with the boys while I unpacked. I so looked forward to their help and support.

~

We loved living in San Diego. Our new neighborhood was active with young families, and kids for Ryan to play with. The economy was booming. Mark picked and chose the jobs he wanted, the ones he knew he could make good money on, and we were back on our feet. The real estate market was going crazy. People camped out at new housing developments just to get on the waiting list for one of the new houses. When the houses got to a certain stage of development, if you didn't put your money down, you were off the list, and the next person had the opportunity to make the down payment on their new home. Of course, Mark wanted to take advantage of this escalating market, and make some money. The agent, who had sold us the "red" house, managed to get us on the list for a house to be built in a new subdivision in the neighboring community of Rancho Bernardo. When the time came to put money down, we had decided to go forward, as the price of homes continued to skyrocket, and the new house was going to be really nice. Ryan was in kindergarten, and I didn't think it would be too disruptive for him to change schools at this stage. We would be able to move before he started first grade. We watched the house being built and were able to choose the countertops and flooring we wanted, and meet some of the other buyers, who all seemed like nice people.

When the time came to move, we sold the "red" house for a tidy profit, $60,000 in just one year, and moved into the nicer, larger, more elegant Rancho Bernardo House. Again there were lots of kids, very much a family neighborhood, and this is where we would stay for the next twelve years. This is the house where the boys were raised, going to school with all the neighborhood kids. My childhood was spent in one place, and I very much wanted the same for my kids. A major part of our family life, both good and bad, took place in that house. As luck would have it, about ten boys, near my kids' ages, lived within a block or so. They were everywhere, in and out of all our houses, having sleepovers, riding bikes and skateboards, and just being boys. There were a few stay-at-home moms, including me, so there was usually someone stationed outside in front of our houses, reading a book or visiting with other neighbors, keeping an eye on what the boys were up to.

Our little family, Mark, Ryan, Aaron, and me.

~

Mark and I were comfortable with our roles, him as bread winner - which he was very good at - and me as hands-on parent, which I hope I was good at. If I knew what I know now, I would have done some things differently, but I did the best I could, putting the boys first in all my decisions. We helped each other out as time permitted, and for the most part, we did pretty well. Of course there were many problems, challenges, and tragedies, like with all families, but also many happy memories and a lot of love. Christmas and birthdays were big events. We probably spoiled the kids somewhat, but if that is the worst thing we did, I am okay with it.

Ryan had struggled with asthma since he was about three, but with medication and close monitoring, we managed it pretty well. In first grade he started having other problems - not sleeping, being withdrawn at school, and generally sad. We didn't understand what a little boy, with a loving family, lots of friends, and a nice home, could be sad about, but sad he was. The hardest part was not being able to sleep, because he would keep us all awake, making life very difficult. My poor little boy, I just wanted him to be happy. We went from pediatrician, allergy specialist, psychologist, to psychiatrist, on a regular basis, but the only diagnosis they agreed on was depression. At six-years-old, my little guy took antidepressants, which helped somewhat, but something else that we just couldn't uncover persisted.

Traveling a lot again, doing jobs in other states and other parts of California, Mark made an effort to be home as much as possible, but I was on my own much of the time. Antidepressants didn't help Ryan sleep. He would come to me for comfort almost every night, and I would try everything to get him to sleep, but we were both up long hours, night after night. Some nights he would wake Aaron and persuade him to come and sleep in his room on his top bunk, and even though Aaron wanted to sleep in his own bed, he would go, just to quiet Ryan. Finally, at my breaking point after several years of fragmented sleep, I made an appointment with Ryan's psychiatrist for myself, mainly to make sure he understood what was going on at home, and possibly to get help for myself, as I was becoming a basket case, desperate for a good night's sleep.

I explained to the psychiatrist what our nights were like. He asked questions and listened carefully. I think Ryan was ashamed to open up to him and his other doctors, so they really didn't know what was going on. At some point during our conversation, a light went on in the doctor's head. "I think I know what is wrong with Ryan," he exclaimed. "It sounds like Obsessive-Compulsive Disorder." I was not familiar with OCD, and after the doctor understood Ryan's need to have all of his stuffed animals arranged precisely in his bed before he could think about sleeping, it all fell into place. "I am going to change his medication, and I think he will be much better," he assured me. Ryan was depressed because he was trying to cope with, and hide all of his obsessions and compulsions. I had high hopes that the new medication would help us.

My prayers were answered when just two days after starting the new medication, he bounded into my bedroom early in the morning after sleeping all night with an ear-to- ear grin, exclaiming, "Mom, I didn't have to arrange my animals last night. I don't have to spin around in a circle every time I get up." This was the first time I had seen my son truly happy in the last three years. We hugged and I thought I would burst with joy for him and for our family, who had all been suffering along with Ryan.

A week or two later I went to Back-to-School Night, and Ryan's teacher sought me out right away. "What is going on with Ryan? He is suddenly so animated, raising his hand to answer questions, and being social with the other students. He is like a new person!" I explained about the new diagnosis and medication, and she was genuinely happy that we had found help for her student whom she had known was unhappy.

MARK HANDS

Mark and I were dedicated parents. We had a couple of date nights a month, otherwise we focused on earning a good living, and raising our family. When Aaron was about three and Ryan eight, we decided they were old enough to be left with my mother while we took an adults-only vacation. We had not been able to ski much while the kids were so little, so we opted for a trip to Beavercreek, at Vail, Colorado, to celebrate our anniversary in February. I booked a slope-side condominium in the village at Beavercreek, and we arranged for my mother to spend the week with the boys at our home. Her mother, my Grandma Rose, was staying with her at the time, so she came with Mom to spend the week with her great-grand sons. Once the grandmas settled in and got briefed on the boys' schedules, Mark and I jetted off to the Rocky Mountains.

The village at Beavercreek was all that we expected, and our condo was elegant and spacious, with a view of the slopes. What a perfect spot for a child free vacation! Unfortunately, there had not been snow in the last week or two, and the snow conditions were not ideal, hard packed and icy, but we didn't care. We were pretty good skiers and used to all kinds of conditions. To make the most of our time at Vail, we decided we would rent demo skies to try some of the latest equipment.

Mark found the perfect skis to rent, and the technician assured him his form on the slopes would be greatly improved with these high performance skies. Disappointingly they did not have any of their best skies in my size, but I did not want to be outdone by Mark, so I rented a pair, even though they were too long for me. I would try them in the morning, and if I didn't like them I could always exchange them, or ski on my own skies, the ones Mark referred to as *dogs*. We took the skies to our locker and then strolled through the wintery village to explore and find a place for dinner. Afterwards we soaked in the hot tub before turning in to rest for a great day of skiing.

If you want to ski with Mark, be prepared to be the first out in the morning, and last off the mountain at the end of the day. I could have come out later and met up with him somewhere, but I was anxious, too, so there we were, standing at the chairlift, waiting for it to start running. The sky was clear, the air was cold, and the snow was as hard as concrete. Up we went for a warmup run to get the feel of our unfamiliar skies.

Finally, I caught up with Mark, who had had a great run, while I struggled to control the too-long skis on the ice. "I am turning these skis in for something else," I reported, at the bottom. "They are too much for me to handle."

"You haven't given them a chance!" Mark exclaimed. "Keep them for a while, and see if you get used to them."

Maybe he's right, I thought, and off we went back up the mountain. After a time, I began to get the hang of the longer skies and discovered that I could actually go really fast on them, much faster than on my *dogs*. They also enabled me to better handle the hard, icy runs. They were still a challenge for me, but I was having fun, and we skied for several hours until Mark decided he wanted to progress to the double black diamond runs. My legs were starting to tire, so we split up and I skied alone; there were not many other skiers because of the icy conditions. Even though I was getting tired, it was so peaceful, having the runs all to myself, that I continued to ski, reveling in the chill air, inhaling the smell of the pines, and skiing really well. When the light began to flatten, I decided it was time to head back to the condo, so I took a different run that would bring me down near our locker. My *last* run was fantastic! I killed it! I skied like I had never skied before, fast and clean. Exhilarated and forgetting I had planned to quit early, I went right back to the chair lift to have another go. Feeling proud of myself, I wished that Mark had been there to see me skiing so well; however, as I rode the lift back up the mountain, I realized my thighs and calves were burning. *I should have gone in*, I worried. *Now I have no choice but to ski down with these worn-out legs.*

The chair I was riding took me way up, allowing some time for my legs to recover. Still, I knew I should call it a day and slowly make my way to our locker. Once off the lift, I saw the sign directing me to the village where our condo was located, but then I saw the arrow pointing to that awesome run I had just aced. *Which way should I go?* I pondered, as I cruised along the ridge while the snow turned a blue-gray in the lengthening shadows. *This way takes me in, but this way takes me to that thrilling run*, I thought, when suddenly my ski caught in a rut and pulled to the right, while my other ski refused to respond to my worn out muscles - and in what felt like slow motion, my legs pulled further and further apart, until finally, they stretched as far as they could stretch, and I heard a pop, and then another pop, as my legs buckled inward. I fell face first onto the hard snow, with both my skies still attached to my boots, leaving me helpless to do anything but lie there. *Oh my gosh, I am stuck here in the snow being pulled apart like a wishbone. Can I move? Am I hurt? Maybe I can right myself and ski down.* While I was assessing my predicament, a skier, who had seen me go down, rushed over asking, "Do you need some help? Are you okay? That looked like a nasty fall."

"I think I am okay," I responded, "If you can just help me get my skies off, so I can get up."

He got my skies off and helped me sit up, and then told me to stay put while he went for the ski patrol. I agreed, and he skied off in a flash. While I waited, I wondered if I actually needed the ski patrol. *Maybe I should put my skies back on and ski down. I seem to be all right. I am not in any extreme pain.* I was a little stunned, maybe in shock, but within minutes two ski patrollers showed up with their transport basket in tow. They quickly removed their skies and began to examine my legs, asking questions as they felt for obvious signs of injury. "Are you in pain," they asked. "Did you hear a popping sound?"

"Yes, I did," I responded. "I heard two popping sounds. But I am not in much pain. I could probably ski down."

"No, you won't be skiing down. We are taking you to the Vail Valley Hospital to be checked out. Are you here with someone; how can we contact them?" they asked, as they lifted me into the basket and proceeded to wrap and bind me like a mummy.

"My husband is here skiing. His name is Mark Haines."

"We will leave a message for him to contact the ski patrol at the base of all the lifts, so he will know you have been hurt."

Bound so tight I was completely helpless, I took a long, harrowing ride, head first, down the face of the mountain. *I hope these guys knows what they are doing,* I thought, as my rescuers maneuvered the basket down the steep, slick run. I still did not think

I was really hurt, but I guessed it was a good idea to get checked out. Once we reached the bottom, I was lifted, basket and all, into the back of an ambulance, and off we went to the emergency room.

Meanwhile, Mark skied to his heart's content, but also noticed a sign reading *Mark Hands, call the ski patrol*. After seeing it a few times, he wondered if he was Mark Hands, but decided probably not and continued to ski until, as usual, he was the last one on the mountain. Upon reaching our locking, he was surprised that my skies were not there. *Uh oh*, he thought, *I guess I am Mark Hands*.

On our way to the hospital, the ski patrollers told me the popping sounds I had heard indicated snapped or torn ligaments, and again asked if I was in pain. By this time my right knee had begun to swell, but no, I was not in much pain.

The X-rays confirmed I had blown out my anterior cruciate ligament (ACL), and partially torn my medial collateral ligament (MCL). I blamed myself, because the skis I rented were too long for me, and I should have known better. No question, surgery was needed; we just had to decide if I wanted to fly home with my leg in a brace for the surgery, or have it done there. According to the pharmacist and our concierge, some of the best orthopedic surgeons practiced there. We reasoned that we had the condominium rented for the entire week, the kids were safe with the grandmas, so I was put on the surgery schedule for the following afternoon. We slowly made our way back to our condo where, despite ice-packs, I watched my knee swell to the size of a honeydew melon.

I checked into the hospital the next afternoon to find several other torn ligaments, broken legs, and dislocated shoulders ahead of me. Finally, at around 8:00 p.m., my turn came, and I was wheeled down the corridor, leaving Mark to wait. The next thing I knew I woke in my room, groggy and uncomfortable, with my knee strapped into a continuous passive motion machine (CPM), which prevents the knee from getting stiff, bending and flexing, bending and flexing, while I lay on my back. For pain management the doctor had left the epidural used during surgery in place, leaving my legs mostly numb. The nurse got me settled in, informing me it was near midnight, that the surgery had gone well, and that I should just rest. Not having much choice, I tried to relax and sleep.

Sleep came and went, and in what seemed like an hour or two, the physical therapist was at my bedside, waking me up. "Wake up Ms. Haines, it is time to go to therapy," the therapist cheerfully announced.

"I think you have the wrong patient. I just had surgery a few hours ago," I told him. I couldn't imagine why I would be going to therapy so soon.

"No, you are scheduled for a 7:00 a.m. session, and then again this afternoon at 3:00 p.m. Come on, I will help you out of bed."

Get out of bed? I thought. *I can barely lift my head, and I can't feel my legs.* "I can't do it," I told the therapist. "I still have the epidural in my back, and I am numb."

"I know, we will wheel your IV stand along with us. Let me unfasten the CPM, and I will help you up."

Somehow I made it to a standing position, but with no feeling in my legs, and my feet feeling like little balls, being pricked with a thousand needles, attached to my ankles, I did not believe I could walk. "Here are your crutches, let's get going. I know it is hard, but the sooner you start using your leg, the sooner you will heal."

I resigned myself to this torture and began to make my way down the corridor wobbling on the crutches, breaking out into a cold sweat as I struggled to make my legs obey. I teetered on my feet, which didn't feel like feet at all, but like round stubs. Just when I thought I was going to pass out, the evil therapist announced we would be going through an obstacle course on the way to our session. I looked ahead, and to my horror I saw a wooden platform with stairs on either side. "Are you kidding me? You can't be serious? You expect me to climb those stairs and then come down the other side?" *God help me*, I thought.

"Yes, you can do it. I will help you."

"Easy for you to say," I responded. "You have no idea how hard this is for me." By this time, I was near tears.

"Here we are, up you go."

I made it back to my bed, feeling as if I had been through a torture treatment instead of therapy, still marveling that they were making me get up so soon. I immediately began to worry about my next session. I soon came to the conclusion that my difficulty walking was due to the fact that the epidural would not allow me to control my legs. When the nurse came in, I told her I wanted it taken out as soon as possible, definitely before my next therapy session. She explained it was up to the doctor, but she would let him know my wishes. When he came in later, he reluctantly agreed, thinking I would regret having it removed since it was there to mask the pain. He was wrong. Once I got the feeling back in my legs, I was able to function so much better. Yes, postoperative pain remained, but it was nothing compared to walking around on what felt like baseballs for feet.

After that traumatic first day I felt better and better, and relaxed while my knee healed. On the fourth day, I was released to the condo, and while Mark got a few more days of skiing, I watched TV and read a couple of books.

By the time the week came to an end, I got around pretty well, and was instructed to see an orthopedic doctor at home for follow-up care. Not the vacation that I had hoped for, the last few days served as a restful time for a busy mom.

FAMILY ADVENTURES

San Diego is a great place for family fun. On weekends we visited Sea World, the famous San Diego Zoo, or the Wild Animal Park, or we took an occasional trip to Disneyland, and of course to the beach. We would pack our minivan with beach towels, boogie boards, umbrellas and all the necessities for a sunset barbecue. Often we met our good friends, Mark and Julie, who lived in our neighborhood and had two boys, Zach and Andrew, our sons' ages. The four boys entertained themselves, playing in the surf and sand, allowing the adults to relax and enjoy a good book and take long beach walks. In the evening we would gather together and enjoy a great barbecue, watching the sun go down behind the ocean in a blaze of glory. We shared carefree, picture perfect summer days.

Aaron on boogie board, and Ryan, enjoying the surf.

One Sunday we had planned to drive to Disneyland after Mass. When we got home, blinking on our telephone recorder caught our eye. Mark pushed the button and we heard David's - Mark's youngest brother - halting voice.

"Call me at Mom's as soon as you can. I have bad news, it's really bad." Mark grabbed the receiver and dialed his mother's number.

"What is it, what has happened?" Mark asked, when Dave answered his call.

"It's Bobby, he's dead. He crashed his car into a tree last night." He sobbed the news to a stunned, confused Mark.

"It can't be, I just talked to him, he was moving to Florida," he argued, as the news began to sink in and he began to sob.

After he hung up, the boys and I gathered around to learn the details of this tragedy. Bobby, the middle of the three brothers, had been living in Maui, working as a manager for the beautiful Hyatt Regency Hotel there. He had recently accepted a job offer in Florida, thinking it was time to return to the mainland. The night before his flight off the islands, while demonstrating the merits of his prized Corvette to a prospective buyer, he lost control of the car and slammed head-on into a tree, killing them both instantly.

What a shock it was to lose our young, talented, thirty-four-year-old brother so suddenly! We all sat together on the couch crying, even two-year-old Aaron, who really didn't understand what happened, trying to come to terms with our loss. Mark's mother and stepfather, were inconsolable. I began preparing us for our trip to the Bay Area to be with family and help with the arrangements. A large out-pouring of support from family and friends helped get us through this tough time. Bobby was well loved, and it showed with the number of people who joined us for his services. Mark and David were able to support each other, but I don't think Lucy, their mother, ever got over losing her middle son. Her health began to fail after Bobby's death, and she was never well again.

CAMPING

Mark and I had both loved camping. We camped with our families when we were young, and continued sharing our love of the great outdoors after we married. Unlike us, our boys claimed they didn't like camping. They would fuss and complain while we packed the gear for our summertime campouts. Once we got to the mountains, though, they did have some fun. They would never admit to it, but at times they enjoyed themselves; I have the pictures to prove it. Camping was a lot of work, so when we went, I wanted all my senses satisfied and my soul nourished. In my quest for the perfect campground I called the forest service offices, quizzing the rangers, and relaying all of my requirements for a successful campout, including no crowds and in a remote location, old-growth forest, a river stocked with trout, hiking trails, bathrooms, and showers. I realized this Shangri-La would be nearly impossible to find in crowded California, but I persevered. Eventually a ranger recommended a campsite in the Sequoia National Forest, not in the national park itself, but in the forest. The national forest campgrounds are more remote and less developed than the parks themselves, which are reservation only. She explained this campground was not only in the forest, it was in a grove of giant sequoias, and on a river that was stocked with trout twice a week. Only fourteen campsites, reservations would not be required because of the remote location. She said it was a hidden treasure. There were no showers or flush toilets, but otherwise it sounded perfect.

After a long six-hour drive, we arrived at Belknap Campground, set in the midst of the McIntyre Grove of giant sequoias. We were in awe. The sequoias were gigantic, and being in their presence was humbling. Everything about this spot could not have been more majestic, pines of all types and sizes, a beautiful river spanned by wooden foot bridges, and serene hiking trails. The best part of my discovery was that there were not many people. It became our go-to campground for years to come. Its lack of showers served as its only drawback. I solved this problem by devising a homemade shower, building a 6-by-6-foot frame of PVC pipes, and hanging shower curtains all around. The PVC pipes could be taken apart and stored in a tent bag, along with the shower curtains for easy packing. For water I bought a large solar water bag with a shower nozzle attached, let it sit in the sun all afternoon until the water was toasty warm, then had Mark hang it in a tree above my homemade shower stall. Each evening we all enjoyed a warm, private shower, before climbing into our sleeping bags. The boys were in hysterics the evening Mark lost his towel on his way from the shower, "streaking" across our campsite to the tent. I should have patented and marketed my simple yet ingenious design, as it worked perfectly. Over the years, versions of my camp shower came on the market, but none as functional as mine.

One summer we arrived at Belknap camp on a hot afternoon, and after setting up the tents, my shower, and the cooking facilities, Mark and the boys grabbed their poles and headed to the river to catch some fresh trout for dinner. I took the opportunity to pull one of our inflatable beds outside in the shade of the pine trees and relax for a while with my book. *Awwww*, I thought, as I relaxed in the afternoon breeze with the singing and chirping of birds all around. *But wait, what is that rustling sound coming from the hillside beside our camp. Probably squirrels*. I didn't bother to look up, but then, once again, the rustling distracted me, and I looked up, and there, on the hillside next to our camp, was the source of the disturbance. A bear foraging around in the brush about ten yards from where I was lying. I panicked and jumped up, thinking to cross the dirt road to where the host camped, but then realized I had taken my boots off, because the rocks and twigs dug into my bare feet. "Ouch, ouch, ouch, I need my shoes." The bear watched my every move, so I decided to forget the shoes, and I quickly but gingerly made my way to the camp host's trailer. "There is a bear at my camp across the way!" I exclaimed. The host grabbed his rifle and went stomping across the road. "Wait, you are not going to shoot the bear, are you?"

"I will if I have to. You better stand back."

Oh no, the poor bear, I worried as I hobbled my way back across the road. When the bear saw the rather large camp host charging towards him, he took off up the hill and out of sight, with the rifle-toting host right behind him. I did not see either one of them for a while, but eventually the host came back, saying he figured the bear was long gone and we were safe for now. Thank goodness the over-zealous host did not feel the need to shoot at the bear. I would have felt awful.

Good morning, Aaron.
Camping at Belknap camp in Sequoia National Forest

Ryan, fishing for our dinner.

A SECOND SCARE

During this busy time, I once again noticed a persistent tickle or tingling that was similar to what I had experienced with the cancerous mole on my face, drawing my attention to a small mole on my right forearm. Upon examination, my new dermatologist, who was aware of my history of melanoma, assured me it was not cancer, and nothing more than an itchy mole, which did not need to be removed. I questioned him as to how he could be so certain by just looking at it. He condescendingly informed me that he was the one with the education and experience and knew what melanoma looked like. I left his office somewhat relieved, but slightly uneasy. After a couple of weeks, I noticed the little mole on my arm bleeding a little bit. My earlier education had taught me this was not a good sign. I went back to the doctor, asking him to remove the mole. He thought I was being overly cautious, but agreed to take it off. A few days later he called me at home with the news that the pathology report confirmed melanoma. Humbled and embarrassed, he could not apologize enough for not recognizing that the mole should have been removed immediately. He requested I come in as soon as possible.

The cancer was a little deeper this time, borderline between Stage I and II. At Stage II, the cancer can enter the blood stream and spread throughout the body. Once this happens, survival rates diminish greatly. A little more surgery was required to achieve margins clear of any affected cells. Being a glass-half-full kind of person, I assumed borderline meant it was not quite Stage II, and that more extensive surgery would be the end of it. With clear margins, a new jagged scar on my right forearm, and a busy life to get back to, I once again put melanoma out of my mind.

AARON!!!

Since Mark and I loved our ski trips so much, it was only natural that we would get our boys out on the slopes at a young age, so that eventually we could all ski together. It was so much more work with children, carrying their gear in addition to our own, and making sure they kept dry and warm enough. But we felt it was worth it, for when the time came, we would be schussing down the slopes together as a family. For the first couple days of each trip we would enroll the boys in ski school, and then at the end of the trip we would all ski together. They learned pretty quickly and did well, unless it got too cold or the snow fogged their goggle lenses, or whatever problem arose on any particular day - and many occurred. Like the year we all went to the beautiful resort at Telluride, high in the mountains of Colorado. The ski mountain there is quite steep and suited to more advanced skiers. The boys had their first day of lessons, and Ryan, being more cautious, struggled keeping up with the "older kid's" class. At the end of the first day he said he was sick. In fact, he got real sick. I kept him in the next two days, and I realize now that he had been suffering from altitude sickness. He recovered and we were soon back out on the slopes. My sweet little Aaron, in the meantime, was having a blast. Only about five at the time, that steep, rugged mountain did not frighten him one little bit. He would bomb straight down the run, scaring us to death. We had to rein him in so he didn't fly off the side of the mountain. Yikes, skiing with kids is challenging!

Another time we were skiing at Park City, Utah, and the temperature had dropped below zero and was not warming up much during the day. One 10-degree-below-zero morning, we piled on the thermal underwear, turtlenecks, jackets, and hats, and headed to Deer Valley to brave the cold day. It had snowed about five inches during the night, and, as usual, Mark wanted to make first tracks on the new snow. Even with the kids we were some of the first people in line for the chairlift. Mark and Ryan headed up, and Aaron and I stood in line for the chair right behind them. As our chair came around, the lift operator turned to do something and did not brush the accumulated snow off of the seat. We had no choice but to sit right in it. As we began the long accent, I worried that our bottoms would be wet when we got off the chair and knew that if skinny, little Aaron got cold, our day would not go well. I lowered the guard bar on the chair, and then I decided I would try to get the snow out from under us. I was wiping it away from under Aaron, and he raised up a little so I could get my hand under him - and before I could react, he slipped right under that bar and down he fell to the snow covered ground far below, landing right on his back. Oh my God! He hit the snow with a thud. I screamed as I climbed higher and higher away from him. "My son, my son fell off the chair!" I yelled to whoever could hear me. What could I do? I thought of jumping off the chair myself, but it climbed higher and higher, until I could no longer see him.

Mark in the chair ahead heard my screams and surmised what had happened, with me screaming and Aaron not in the chair. We both freaked out, because there was nothing we could do but ride the chair to the top of the mountain. The people on the chairs behind us yelled messages up to us that the ski patrol had got to him, and that he seemed to be all right. That was somewhat reassuring, but I could not get to the top soon enough. The instant Mark got to the top, he told Ryan to wait for me and he took off, racing to the bottom to get to Aaron. When I finally got to the top, I saw Ryan waiting there. "Come on Ryan, let's get down there!" The three of us had never skied so fast.

As Ryan and I clicked out of our skies, we spotted Mark being escorted to the first-aid office, and we sprinted across the snow, leaving our skies behind. We all entered the office together, and there sat Aaron, enjoying a cup of steaming hot chocolate. "I got to ride on a snow mobile!" he excitedly exclaimed. We all grabbed him and hugged him close. Thank goodness he was not hurt! I still feel guilty about that, but I didn't want him to start the day wet and cold.

The boys and I on the slopes.

SUPER BOWL HERE WE COME

Mark and I are National Football League fans. We always watch the games on Sunday and Monday night together. It was our favorite past-time during the cold, autumn, Alaskan weekends. Alaska did not have a home team, so we rooted for the teams from back home: The San Francisco 49ers and the Oakland Raiders. When we relocated to San Diego in 1988, we realized now we had a home team that we could go watch in person. One of the first things we did as San Diegans was to purchase season tickets for the San Diego Chargers. They were nosebleed seats, but that was all that was available. We had two tickets, and Mark thought it would be something he and Ryan could do together. Aaron was still a baby, so I stayed home with him. Our seats were so high in the stadium, that five-year-old Ryan would get bored and fidgety, so soon we got a baby-sitter, and I joined Mark for the Sunday home games. We kept a watch on tickets sales, and after a year or two we upgraded, purchasing four really good season-ticket seats.

After a time, we realized some of the contractors Mark worked with - also fans, some of them long-time season-ticket holders - were also at the games and we were invited to join their elaborate pre-game tailgate parties. On the West Coast our games usually start at 1:00 p.m., so the tailgating begins as early as 8:00 or 9:00 in the morning. We usually arrived about 10:00, joining the more die-hard fans who were already firing up their grills and flipping open their third or fourth beers.

These fun game-day get-togethers continued for several years. We cheered on the San Diego Chargers, usually a less than stellar team, and shared great food, drink, and companionship. After a decade of some dismal seasons for the Chargers, in the early 1990s they actually put a good team on the field. As the 1994 season progressed, to our dismay and delight, the Chargers continued to win. Against all odds they won the American Football Conference title and were headed to Miami, Florida, to compete against the San Francisco 49ers in Super Bowl XXIX. The city was ecstatic. Charger banners and colors were on display all over town. Everyone wore their Charger championship gear and planned epic Super Bowl parties. Our group of fans would all attend our annual Super Bowl party, with the added bonus of having our home team participating in the big game.

During this time, Mark was doing apartment renovations in Texas. He flew out early Monday morning and returned home Friday night. It was not an ideal situation, but he is not one to pass up an opportunity to make good money. The week before the Super Bowl, I was rushed and stressed as usual, running Mom's taxi service for seven-year-old Aaron, and eleven-year-old Ryan, with any combination of piano lessons, sports practices and games, and Boy Scout meetings. Once we finally arrived home, it was time for dinner, homework, bath time, etc. At some point during these hectic evenings, I would walk up the street to our mailbox to collect our late-arriving mail. On the Thursday night before Super Bowl

Sunday, walking home from the mailbox, I noticed a letter from the Chargers. *What can this be?* I wondered. I opened the letter and read: *Your name has been drawn in the lottery of season ticket holders for Super Bowl tickets. Your tickets can be picked up at the ticket office Friday after 9:00 am.*

I did not know about the lottery and had not given a second thought to going to the game in Miami. *But we have tickets! Tickets for Sundays game, and it's Thursday evening. But it is the Super Bowl! Can we do it?* I immediately called Mark and told him the news. He was coming home Friday night, and I told him I would go to the ticket office in the morning and see what I could find out. He said he would look into flights from Texas, and maybe we could meet in Miami.

The next morning, I got the kids off to school and headed down to the stadium ticket office to find long lines of people just as befuddled as I was. I found the line to pick up tickets and struck up a conversation with the people around me. I learned that it was next-to-impossible to get a flight into Miami, or to get accommodations. Then someone told us she had heard there was a travel agent in the next room who had packages available. Apparently the Pittsburgh Steelers had been expected to be going to the Super Bowl. When the Chargers pulled off an upset, Pittsburgh travel agents had travel packages from Pittsburgh to Miami that they were stuck with. They quickly contacted agents here in San Diego, and redirected some chartered airline flights to fly out of San Diego, so that Charger fans could use them. We all agreed that after we picked up our tickets, we would head over there and get signed up.

A little while later I held the highly sought after, hologram designed, Super Bowl tickets thinking, *I'm going to the Superbowl. This is amazing.* However, I had a lot to do in the next twelve hours if we were going to be on one of those charter flights. While standing in line at the travel agent's desk, I called Mark letting him know that he would have to be back in San Diego that night and be ready to be at the airport again by 11:00 p.m. to catch a midnight charter. He said he could do it and was glad I was getting us on the charter, because he was not able to get a flight from Texas to Miami all weekend. I stepped up to the travel agent and bought the weekend package including the flights, hotel room for two nights, and some pregame parties. All my new friends I had just met in line would be on the same flight and staying in the same hotel. We were all in it together. I raced out of there to begin making preparations for the weekend.

Our friend, Julie, agreed to keep the boys and was very excited we were going to the big game. I also called our tailgating friends who were hosting the Super Bowl party, to let them know we could not be there, because we would be at the game. "What?" she exclaimed! "You're going to the Super Bowl! Wait until I tell everyone." I packed the boys weekend things, packed a bag for myself and Mark, picked up the boys from school - who were very excited to be spending the weekend with their friends - dropped them off at Julie's, and then returned home, prepared to pick Mark up at the airport at 8:00 p.m.

The bags packed, I whipped up a quick dinner we could eat on the way out, and then headed down to pick up Mark, whose plane was luckily on-time. I spotted him outside of baggage claim and pulled up to get him. On the way home I filled him in on our schedule. First we had to get home, have a bite to eat, grab our things, and then turn around and get back to the airport within two hours. He was tired, but excited that we had been chosen in the lottery for Super Bowl tickets.

After a frenzied day for both of us, we finally settled in our seats on the charter, at midnight Friday night. We thought we might get some sleep on the five-hour flight, but it was not to be. Everyone onboard was a Charger fan, and the party began as soon as we took off. The flight was noisy, but a fun start to our weekend. When we arrived in Miami, we were shuttled to our less than luxurious hotel, which was actually on the beach.

The whole weekend was fantastic. The NFL sure knows how to host a party. The whole town was one big party. We did it all, the NFL Experience, late night clubbing, special parties for our charter, and finally, on Sunday evening, the big game. After entering the stadium, we climbed to the top of a spiral staircase and watched the rich and famous fly into a helicopter pad below us. Inside the stadium, the air sparked with electricity. We took in all of the spectacular pregame entertainment. Finally arriving at our seats, we found souvenir seat cushions and bags of gifts filled with novelties, all adding to this one-of-a-kind experience. The whole weekend was magic, with the one exception of the Chargers getting pounded by the mighty San Francisco 49ers. We had expected that to happen, so we did not let that put a damper on our weekend. After the game we went out on the town with some of our new friends, experiencing the famed Miami nightlife. When we woke up Monday morning, we felt a little rough, but were still on the high of all we had enjoyed the last two days. We managed to mosey out to the beach, where we found a plastic table and chairs, and sat and let the sea air revive us. The flight home was quiet and smooth. When we got home, we were the envy of all of our football buddies, and they had a right to be envious, because it was an awesome event!

ME AGAINST THE COLORADO RIVER

Aaron became a Boy Scout after earning his Arrow of Light in the Cub Scouts. One of his first major scouting adventures was a three-day canoe trip down the mighty Colorado River, camping along the way. Designed as a father-son event, Mark and Aaron prepared diligently. They took canoeing lessons and purchased waterproof duffle bags to keep their camping gear dry as they navigated the strong currents of the Colorado.

Eleven-year-old Aaron (all seventy pounds of him) was proud and excited to be going on such a grownup outdoor expedition. The morning of their afternoon departure, he was bursting to get the school day over with, so he could get on the river and use his newly acquired skills. I dropped him off at school and returned home to find Mark finishing up the packing and checking his list. Not as excited as Aaron, he was still being a good sport. "I hope we have all the supplies we need. Everything is water tight. And our tent has a waterproof rainfly if it should rain," he assured me, as he finished securing the bags. Then the phone rang - and suddenly, the canoe trip was at risk of being canceled at the last minute.

"What is it?" I asked, as I heard Mark questioning his brother. Once again it was David, calling with bad news. Their grandmother, our beloved Noni, was critically ill and asking for Mark. Dave, who was an MD by this time, informed us that she did not have much time left. She had been a major part of Mark's life, babysitting him while his mom worked, and spoiling and fawning over him, to the chagrin of her other six grandchildren. We both felt that he should go and be with her.

"But what about Aaron? He will be so disappointed," he sighed. "We have put so much into preparing for this trip. What should I do?"

Naturally I had begun tossing solutions around in my head ever since Mark had been on the phone. "You go up to be with Noni, and I will go on the canoe trip with Aaron. Everything is ready; how hard can it be to float down the river and camp beside it at night? I will call Julie and see if Ryan can stay with them," I offered.

"Are you sure?" Mark asked. "Do you think you can handle the canoe?"

"I am sure I can do it. Aaron can give me a crash course before we launch. Go ahead and pack your suitcase, and don't worry about us." I wasn't as confident as I let on, but I would, and still will, do anything for my boys, all three of them. Let the adventure begin!

As I sat in the car waiting for Aaron to get out of school, I wondered if he would be disappointed. I knew that Karen, his homeroom teacher, was also going with her husband and two sons, so I knew I would not be the only mom, and hopefully Aaron wouldn't be embarrassed. As he climbed into our minivan, I broke the news to him, and he seemed to be fine with it. Of course being such a sweetheart, he wouldn't have let me know if he was disappointed.

At the meeting place where we joined the caravan to the river, I explained that I would be taking Mark's place, and everyone agreed it would be fine. I was so glad to have Karen along to confide in. We had gotten to know each other since I did some volunteering in her classroom, and she was very fond of Aaron. It would have been an uncomfortable outing if I had been the only female; however, these boys were young enough to consider a mom just as good as a dad. Soon the gear was loaded, and our journey got underway.

We arrived at our campsite on the river after dark and everyone quickly set up their tents and began preparing their evening meal, while Aaron and I struggled, not knowing what Mark had packed, how to set up a tent, much less in the dark, and what we were expected to contribute to the group.

We finally got our camp set up for the night, with little assistance from anyone (I thought boy scouts were supposed to be helpful), and had sandwiches for dinner. We took so long getting our tent and beds ready that it was too late to fix anything hot. I had Aaron go over the techniques he had learned at his canoeing class with me, and we planned to do some practice in the cove before we set out in the morning. Once we settled in to get some sleep, I knew I had bitten off more than I could chew.

The other scouts and dads were up before dawn having breakfast and breaking camp. I guessed we were getting an early start on the river, so I woke Aaron and we quickly had some cereal while the other teams were already packing their canoes.

"Let's get packed, we are way behind," I told Aaron, as he finished his cereal. We began rolling our sleeping bags and trying to stuff them into the rubber duffle bags, which was no easy feat. Then we frantically started dismantling our tent, as we realized the others were prepared to leave.

"We are the last ones," I worriedly told Aaron. "Ask some of your friends to come and help us." He ran off and soon returned with some help, and we managed to get all the equipment stuffed into our big yellow rubber duffle bags. As we half carried, half dragged the heavy bags to our canoe, the other teams launched one after another. We loaded everything in the last canoe and got it in the water, just as the others entered the main river.

"Hurry Aaron, you get in the back and I will get in the front. We don't want to lose sight of the others. The river splits in places, and we don't want to get lost." There was no time for practice, as we began to maneuver out of the cove into the river. "Row, Aaron, row, we have to catch up."

Once we got into the powerful current of the main river, with some hard rowing, we caught up with the others, and were able to finally relax. "Okay," I thought. "We can do this." There were about ten or twelve canoes, and we all cruised along, the boys splashing each other with their oars, enjoying the new and wild surroundings. After a couple of hours, I noticed the lead canoes were pulling to the shore. I instructed Aaron to guide us to the sandy area between the tall, thick, reeds that lined the river on both sides.

We made it to the beach with no problems, and everyone splashed into the river to have a swim and cool off. Once refreshed, we had a snack, reapplied our sunscreen, and climbed back into our canoes. Once again, the *man*-powered canoes were quickly and efficiently back in the pull of the current. Our canoe was also grabbed by a current, but not the one we needed. We were caught in a little whirlpool that pulled us into the reeds, trapping us there, as once again the other rowers disappeared from our view around the bend.

We fought against the pull of the errant current, pushing against our cage of reeds, struggling to free ourselves. What a pair we made, seventy pound Aaron without a muscle on his body, and me, worthless at guiding us anywhere except straight down the river! After what seemed like an hour in captivity, but in reality was probably ten minutes, we were freed from the grip of the reed jungle. Once again we struggled, rowing hard, to catch up with the others. And row we did, but it seemed hopeless when the other canoes were being moved along so quickly by the river, too. I had begun to worry we were on our own when I spotted one of our canoes pulled to the side, and my heart soared. *We are saved*, I thought. One of the dads had taken notice that we were missing, and stopped to wait for us. Bless him. I was so relieved, and we rowed along peacefully and uneventfully the rest of that day. The smooth movement of the massive river with the sun glistening off of it, and with the other canoes gliding silently by, soothed my stress away, and we immersed ourselves in a new-found tranquility. As evening approached, we landed at what would be our campsite for the night.

Once our tents were erected and our tummies were full, some of us took a swim in the still water beside our camp as the desert night was hot and dusty. When we crawled into our sleeping bags at last, we realized we were dead tired. "Tomorrow we will be better prepared," I told Aaron as we drifted off to sleep.

The sound of boys hustling around outside our tent woke me early the next morning. "Oh no, not again!" I thought. "Aaron, wakeup, we can't be last on the river again!"

Determined to be one of the first to be packed and ready that morning, I got Aaron some cereal and immediately began packing. I worked diligently, dismissing offers of coffee and small talk, and was one of the first loading our canoe. None too soon though, our leaders were already pushing off. "Let's go Aaron, we will be at the head of the pack today." And we were, rowing even with the lead canoes, out in the middle of the river to avoid any whirlpools and reed jungles. I felt very comfortable about our position.

As we cruised along I took notice of a small fork off to the right, not giving it much thought, when Aaron exclaimed: "Mom, the others are turning right!"

"What!" *This can't be happening*, I thought. "Turn, turn, try to get over there!"

We gave it a great effort, but because we were in the front and out in the midst of the rivers current, we were swept right by the fork. We watched over our shoulders as the other canoes disappeared again. "What should we do, Mom?" Aaron asked.

I was so discouraged, having messed up again. "I think we should pull off to the side, quit rowing, and go as slowly as possible. I am sure someone saw us miss the turn. They will come after us," I hoped. After a few minutes of sitting there all alone, just the two of us, another canoe appeared. They had missed the turn, too. I was so relieved to not be floating there alone.

The missed turn turned out to be less of a disaster then we had feared. Our new companions informed us that while I was furiously packing our gear that morning, a plan was agreed upon to stop for ice-cream at a restaurant reachable from the fork in the river we had missed. The stop was to be a short one, and the others would soon be along. I had not heard a word about it, as I was so determined to be one of the first to launch that morning.

Soon joined by the ice-cream eaters, we continued uneventfully to campsite number three. By the time we reached it, I was so tired I don't even remember setting up our tent or what we ate. I do remember packing in the morning, thinking I would soon be off the river, and home to my shower and bed. Of course the trip couldn't have ended without a little more drama.

Before setting off that last day, our leader described how we would have to cross a busy intersection of the river to get to our landing on the far bank. We were advised to be cautious because there would be a lot of traffic on the river, considering it was Memorial Day. It would take us a short hour to reach, and then we could head for home.

"Are you kidding me!" I exclaimed when I set eyes on this busy intersection. I could not believe we had to row ourselves out into the midst of this congested expanse of water with pleasure boats, jet skis, ski boats pulling skiers, all going in different directions, churning up the water with their wakes. "Aaron, how are we going to survive this?" I cried.

"Just go, Mom. We can do it. Follow the rest of the canoes."

I wasn't going to be left behind again, so we headed into the fray. I seriously feared for us because our canoe was so small compared to all of the motorized water craft flying by us, and rocking our little canoe in their wakes. It was a long way to our landing site, and we rowed with all the energy we had left, dodging and ducking our way through.

When we pulled up to shore for the final time, I thought I was going to cry with relief, having completed what was for me a physical and emotional challenge. We rode home with Karen and her family, all of us sweaty, dusty, and tired, playing road-trip games, and singing silly songs. It appeared I was the only one traumatized by the whole experience.

A SEASON OF LOSS

Mark's mother, Lucy, never recovered from the loss of her middle son, Bobby. While still grieving, she developed a nagging cough that brought her down even more. After a series of doctor appointments and tests, we were devastated, but not surprised, when she was diagnosed with lung cancer. She loved smoking her cigarettes and would never accept that they could harm her. We had begged her for years to stop smoking, but she would not even consider it, and now it was too late for quitting to matter. We flew up to visit her, and one afternoon she told me of a time she had been remembering. While walking through the hospital on the way to an appointment, cigarette in hand (you could smoke in hospitals then), she passed a frail, shrunken, older woman laying on a gurney. The woman reached out to her saying, "Please stop smoking, honey. Look what it has done to me. Lung cancer is a terrible way to die." Lucy told me she had felt sorry for the dying woman, but knew that cancer would never happen to her - it only happened to *other* people - and went right on smoking one cigarette after another.

It took about a year for the cancer to claim her life. The last few months were horrible as she fought for every breath. Mark went up to be with her a few times, and was with her at the very end. She suffered in the worst way, telling Mark as he sat by her bedside one evening, "Maybe tonight will be the night." Mark attempted to comfort her, but he knew the end was near, and, as expected, she passed a few days later. We considered her pretty old at the time, but she was only sixty-four, which today seems so very young. I began to make my preparations to join Mark for his mother's funeral.

~

During this time, I struggled with my recurring depression, something plaguing me since childhood. New medications had recently been introduced, and my doctor-proscribed Prozac. Soon after beginning the medication, I began to feel better, a lot better, better than I had ever felt. Happy all the time, and nothing much phased me. However, the death of a family member was serious enough to awaken some suppressed feelings. I felt some sadness about Lucy's passing, and worried about Mark as I flew to the Bay Area, hoping to arrive in time for the pre-funeral memorial service that evening.

We always stayed at my parents' house when visiting family back home, and even though they were out of town, I had a key and planned for us to stay there for the duration. I arrived with just enough time to change and be on time for the 7:00 p.m. service. I opened my suitcase, took out my black dress, and discovered I had forgotten to pack pantyhose and shoes. *Great*, I thought. *What am I going to wear with this dress? Let me see if Mom has any shoes I can wear. I know she will have pantyhose.*

Mom was about a hundred pounds heavier then I was, and a shoe size bigger. Her pantyhose hung on me, and her shoes flopped off my feet. What could I do? I had no other options.

When I arrived at the chapel, the large crowd sat on both sides of the aisle, and you could have heard a pin drop as the service was about to begin. I shuffled up the aisle to join the family in the front rows, trying to keep my shoes from slapping my heels as they flopped with each step, all the while keeping my legs tightly together in the hope that my mom's queen size pantyhose did not fall down. Thankfully I made it to my seat without anyone noticing my struggle. Relieved to see me, Mark reached for my hand, which he held tightly throughout the memorial. After the service, we all met at Mark's cousin's house, and I immediately took off the oversized shoes and pantyhose, telling our cousins about my predicament. We all had a good, mood-lightening laugh, and found comfort being together.

My medication was doing its job, and I just couldn't be sad. Seeing family and friends we didn't see very often, all together at the same time, made me feel as if I were at one big party, catching up with friends, eating great homemade Italian food, just like a family reunion. I kept having to remind myself that I should at least appear sad and show respect for Mark's mother.

THE FUNERAL

The morning of Lucy's funeral dawned warm and sunny. The chapel service brought a blur of flowers, friends, tears, and hugs. My heart broke for Noni, who had rallied from last year's illness, as she heart-wrenchingly said goodbye to her baby girl. Lucy's open coffin rested behind us as the family left through the side door to the waiting limousines. Noni looked back, reaching for the coffin, and cried, "Goodbye, my baby." My anti-depressant could not protect me from that crushingly sad scene. Losing a child has to be the most difficult of losses no matter how old you - or they - are.

~

Gazing at the springtime hillsides and the fluffy white clouds floating in a clear blue sky, with the warm sun on my shoulders, my medication took over again. I couldn't help but feel exhilarated - until the rows of headstones filled my vision, and I reminded myself where I was, at my mother-in-law's funeral, standing graveside, surrounded by family and friends. Once again, at Queen of Heaven Catholic Cemetery, where both of our families' deceased are buried. *Such a beautiful spot*, I thought, *high in the hills above town, so green and peaceful.* Now my husband's mother was about to join his father and brother, at rest in these beautiful surroundings

Family and friends crowded around the graveside, overflowing beyond the canopy, listening to the service and saying their last goodbyes. Jim, my husband's life-long best friend, stood next to me, looking a little bored. He was very much a part of our family, and was always there for us when times were tough. Jim and I had become close friends through the years, and it was always comforting to have him with us for emotional support. Being some of the only non-Italians in this outwardly emotional family, he and I usually stuck together, considering ourselves the only rational participants at these family gatherings.

While the priest read scriptures, I turned my attention to the other mourners: Lucy's two sons, her mother, and her now widower-husband, Mark's stepdad, who had cared for her through her losing battle with lung cancer, and her nieces and nephews, all enduring the pain of losing a major figure in their lives. Not totally numb to all feelings, my heart ached seeing them in pain. I did care for Mark's mother, but she was not the most lovable person, especially to me. She was the mother of three boys, and I think she resented me to an extent for taking her place in her oldest son's life. She was never warm or loving with me, but then, I would hear that she sang my praises to other members of the family. Always confused by that, I never had a comfortable relationship with her. I was sorry that she had suffered and died relatively young, but never had a strong connection with her. Then I spotted Mark's grandmother, who, on the other hand, adored me, looking so pale and lonely despite being surrounded by loved ones. She had always been my ally, and seeing her grieve for her daughter, did break my heart. How indescribably painful it must be to outlive your child.

My mind began to wander, looking ahead to the socializing to come after the services, again having to remind myself that this was a sad occasion. Apparently Jim's mind had begun to wander, too. He told me later that he was wondering who this poor guy was whose grave we were all trampling over, next to Lucy's freshly dug grave. He looked down at the headstone and was shocked to realize it was my brother's grave. My older brother, who had died of burns suffered in an auto accident about ten years prior, and by coincidence, Mark's mom was now being buried right next to him.

Jim nudged me, and pointed to the headstone all but covered by the grass and dirt from Lucy's grave. And then I saw the name. All the painful memories of losing my beloved older brother came flooding back, and in addition to the emotions already being suppressed by the medication, I suddenly became overwhelmed. I broke down in tears that just kept coming. I had surpassed the limits of the Prozac's effects, and all the feelings I had been numb to were now exposed and raw. I wept for my brother and for all the heartache my family went through during his long, painful journey towards death.

The services had finished, and Jim had gone to comfort Mark, his best friend. As the mourners began to wander off, Mark's sweet Italian aunt, Olivia, saw me in distress and rushed to my side. When I explained why I was so emotional, she took me in her arms, rocking me like a child, as I struggled to gain control. Once I calmed myself, we walked together around the cemetery, visiting other family members' graves, and her genuine compassion touched me deeply. She has always been so very kind to me. We spotted Mark and his brother, David, visiting their dad's and middle brother's graves. They looked so forlorn, standing with their heads bowed like two orphaned children, which they now were. Auntie and I joined them, and we all leaned on each other for comfort as we remembered all the loved ones we had lost. As the cemetery became quiet, we all agreed we should be going to greet the guests who would be arriving at Auntie's house soon.

Just before entering the car, Mark and I looked back just in time to see Lucy's flower-covered coffin being lowered into her waiting grave. I felt Mark whimper and, relieved that I had emerged from the false tranquility of the medication, knew I would be better able to support him and his brother through their grief. I gazed out the window as we drove through the cemetery toward the large wrought-iron gates, and was once again able to appreciate the beauty of this serene and peaceful place where so many of our loved ones now rest. As the intricately scrolled gates closed behind us, I blew a kiss to my big brother, and was finally able to say a sincere goodbye to my mother-in-law, realizing I did love her and was going to miss her very much.

~

Mark's Uncle George, his mother's brother, was the same type A personality, believing smoking would never claim him. Other people got lung cancer, and he continued his habit, even after Lucy's death. I have been told that grief affects the lungs, and I saw it with Lucy, never recovering from Bobby's death, and now Uncle George, about a year after Lucy's death. Was it coincidence that his lungs failed him so soon after his only sibling's death, or was it the result of grief? Whatever the reason, we once again found ourselves at Queen of Heaven Cemetery to bury Noni's only surviving child. She had outlived them both.

GRANDMA ROSE

My mother's mother was the next to leave us. She lived well into her nineties, and what an amazing life she lived! My sister, Julie, and I accompanied our grieving mom to Tecumseh, Oklahoma; Dad was too weak by this time to travel. His rheumatoid arthritis had stabilized, but emphysema now plagued him, leaving him feeble and breathless. He hadn't smoked in thirty years, but his lungs failed him too. We planned to stay after the funeral and clear out Grandma's house, where she had lived for fifty years.

We had always stayed at Grandma Rose and Grandpa Harvey's house when we made our annual summer trip to Oklahoma, so I knew it well. It was very different now that they were both gone, and Uncle Butch, Mom's only brother, who was eleven years younger, lived 40 minutes away in Oklahoma City. The rooms were the same, but felt almost haunted, as this used to be the family hub, always filled with relatives and friends. As we began to go through Grandma's treasures, so much history unfolded before us.

My sister and I were fascinated to learn that our meek, afraid-of-airplanes Grandma, the oldest of six siblings, had pulled her younger brothers from their burning house, and had been the first in town to purchase an automobile after her younger sister lost her baby in the back of a horse-drawn wagon on the way into town to give birth. And surprisingly, she had been one of the first liberated women. She was a legal secretary to the only lawyer in the county, maybe in the state. Grandma traveled with him, staying in whatever room she could rent, usually in someone's attic, and went to Washington, DC, with him, staying months at a time. And to the rest of the family's chagrin and dismay, she kept her job after my mother was born on April 30th, 1929. This was just not done in that time and place. When a woman had a family, her place was in the home. Later that same year, the stock market crashed and as the Depression spread throughout the country, her steady income helped to support the extended family, as it became harder and harder for them to earn a living.

We spent days going through drawers and cabinets. This was too much for Mom to bear, sorting the items to be given away or thrown out. She wanted us to keep everything, which was impractical and unreasonable. Mom did not want to say good-bye to her childhood memories and her beloved parents, clinging to every garment and knick-knack. Uncle Butch took some of the old furnishings, which he later had restored and still uses, but the linens, dishes, and items of everyday life all had to go. To distract Mom, we started asking her to tell us about the items we pulled from shelves and out of trunks, and soon she was lost in reminiscences.

When I discovered boxes of barely used, matched sets of old costume jewelry in Grandma's dresser drawer, I asked Mom what they were. She told us they were gifts given to Grandma by her lawyer-employer's mistress. The mistress would be waiting when they arrived on an out-of-town job, and always offered Grandma a lovely gift of matching necklace and earrings in exchange for her silence. Apparently, Grandma was more worldly than we ever imagined. The mistress knew that Grandma was good friends with her employer's wife. We asked if Grandma ever told the wife, and Mom said she never did, not wanting to break that hurtful news to her friend.

My mom's cedar chest sat in the bedroom I always stayed in at Grandma's, but we had never opened it. Mom, Julie, and I were together the day we decided to open it and discover what was inside. At first look, it appeared to be full of old quilts and blankets; however, as we removed the individual quilts, we discovered something wrapped in the blankets. As we unfurled the first blanket, we found an old doll. By the time we reached the bottom of the chest, we had five worn and tattered dolls. One had been Mom's, a Shirley Temple doll, but she did not know the history of the others, and in fact, had never seen them before. We wondered who's "babies" these were that had been hidden away in the cedar chest all these years - our grandmother's, our great grandmother's? We could only imagine.

NONI

Mark's mothers' mother, Frances Novelli Manos, always known to me as Noni, finally left us after a long and remarkable life. Born in 1900, living through WWI in Italy and WWII in California, she was a wealth of history. I loved hearing her stories of hiding under her father's trench coat, reaching out and stealing bread at the market to keep them alive, and traveling to the United States, alone, by ship, meeting her soon-to-be Greek immigrant husband on that ship. I only wish that I had learned more about her life because, now, much that she experienced is left untold. Noni and my

Grandma Rose were both strong survivors. I learned about being the heart and the rock of a family from these two exceptional examples. They live on through me, as much of the way I live my life is modeled after them.

DAD

Poor Dad was so sick for so long. I have often wondered why such a vibrant, active, fun-loving man, ended up having such debilitating illnesses. His diet was not so good; processed food made up a lot of it, and he did enjoy his share of liquor. In his early fifties, he was diagnosed with rheumatoid arthritis. This disease stopped him in his tracks. His hands began to cripple, and soon he could hardly walk. He was in extreme pain and was mostly bedridden. We tried every remedy: prescription and holistic, to no avail. Nothing we tried offered any relief. After five or six years, he began an unexplained remission, and was once again able to travel and live life. The deformities remained, but his pain level was manageable.

Dad went along like this into his sixties, traveling with friends, regularly attending "meetings" at the Moose Lodge, and visiting us in Alaska, which he thought was the greatest place on earth, even though his arthritis slowed him down. I worked for Wien Air Alaska during some of this time, and I would get my parents passes to travel to Nome, Kotzebue, and Barrow, the northern-most city. He relished these adventures, especially since they went for free. He loved telling people about visiting the Kotzebue National Forest, which consists of one pine tree. But then, gradually, Dad began having trouble breathing.

Someone who has never had asthma takes breathing for granted. Healthy humans breathe automatically without taking notice. But when the process of oxygenating our bodies is compromised, it becomes all-consuming. "I can't catch my breath," he would complain, after struggling to get to the kitchen from the living room. The new diagnosis was emphysema, and soon he was housebound again, relying on my mother's care.

Dad had smoked in the 50s, but stopped at a relatively young age, and we were at a loss to understand why he was afflicted with this "smoker's" disease. Dad's health deteriorated quickly, while he sat in front of the television all day. Just the act of getting up off the couch caused him to gasp for air. He suffered a heart attack, and then, a second, more major heart attack, landing him in the hospital with a pump attached to his heart. He came very close to dying, but recovered enough to come back home. It was November, and for the first time in many years the entire family came together at our childhood home for Thanksgiving. Mark and I and our two boys, together with Tedd and his wife, Lavon, Julie and her significant-other, Dave, and Jerry, all joined Mom and Dad to give thanks and enjoy being together. I remember that Thanksgiving as a happy time, with no family drama and my dad just beaming to have us all around the dining-room table one more time.

Dad's life hung by a thread that he clung to, in hopes of surviving until February, when he and Mom would celebrate their 50th wedding anniversary. My siblings and I quietly planned a surprise party that they knew nothing about. Dad kept reminding us that their 50th anniversary was approaching, and we would shrug and say, "Yes, we know." Acting like we were not very interested.

Somehow, we managed to keep the party a secret, and the night of the event we had Mom and Dad dress up, telling them we were taking them out to dinner. It was a struggle for Dad, but when he arrived at the hall to find all his lifelong friends, family from out-of-town, food, drinks, music and laughter - all to celebrate Mom and Dad - he was overjoyed. We sat them at the head table, overlooking the crowd, while guests took turns sharing stories, pictures, and all the love every person there felt for my parents. It was a night to remember, as we all relived their fifty years together.

Dad passed away two months later in April of 2000. Mom and Jerry were with him and said he passed peacefully. We all knew he had been in pain and discomfort longer than anyone should have to be, and found comfort knowing he was now free. We buried him at Queen of Heaven Cemetery near his first-born son. I hope they were reunited in the afterlife. I miss my Dad.

My dad, Jerome Leo Horbach and me, 1954.

Chapter 9

ILLNESS

The new millennium arrived on the sad note of my father's passing. After a period of relief and then grief, I began to look forward to the new century. A few months after Dad's passing, while showering, I discovered a swelling in the pit of my right arm. It had been nine years since the second primary melanoma site on my right wrist was removed, and I wondered if this could be the melanoma spreading to my lymph nodes. My heart began to race as the voices of the doctors describing what would happen to me if the melanoma entered my bloodstream surfaced in my mind. *But would it reappear nine years later*? I couldn't imagine that it would, and assumed the gland was swollen for another reason.

Not overly alarmed, I made an appointment to have it checked. After the examination, my doctor suggested I see a surgeon. Frightened, but still optimistic, I made the appointment and waited.

The day came to go to the surgeon, and I left for the appointment, eager to get this whole affair behind me. The doctor quickly examined me and said he would schedule a biopsy, and then abruptly headed for the door. I stopped him and told him about my history with melanoma. He froze with his hand on the doorknob. I could almost hear the wheels spinning in his head. After a moment, he informed me that we would not be waiting, and that he would do a needle biopsy right then. The procedure went smoothly, and he said he would have the results in a few days. "Well, good," I thought, eager to get a diagnosis. On the surface, I maintained my optimistic temperament, but deep inside, fear grew.

Mark had already decided that he would be going with me to get the test results. He had been having frank conversations with his brother, Dave, the surgeon, several nights since I discovered the lump. He did not share their discussions with me, but I sensed his concern. I was trying to stay positive, but somehow I knew I needed him to go with me. As soon as the doctor came in, we knew the diagnosis. His face told the story: Melanoma. The cancer had been dormant inside me all this time, and now something had triggered it to grow. In total shock, time seemed to stand still. How do you react to news like this? Mark seemed more shaken then I was. He also knew what a melanoma diagnosis of a lump this large could mean for me.

We drove home in silence, too stunned to speak. I think I lay down when we got home, but I really don't remember. I just remember thinking about my boys. They had just started the new school year, and I couldn't bear to upset their world with this kind of news. Were they old enough to handle this? Would I be able to handle this?

Days later, as we listened to the Oncologist explain my odds of surviving five years, the hope we brought to his office began to fade. He informed us there was no approved treatment for melanoma except for a year of Interferon injections, which some studies suggested could increase my odds slightly. My instincts told me this was not an option to consider. I didn't want to be sick for a whole year from an uncertain treatment, if I only had a maximum of five years left. There had to be something more promising. He suggested I research drug trials.

After the tumor and surrounding lymph nodes were removed, the surgeon explained there were no other nodes testing positive for melanoma. Thank God, I thought. My relief was dashed as he proceeded to inform me that very likely the cancer had spread but was not yet detectable.

How do you sleep? How do you function after a bomb like this is dropped on you? The time between diagnosis and beginning a treatment plan is like a torturous eternity. My nights were fitful and lonely. I think I wore a grove in the carpet where I paced. So many things ran through my mind. *This is not right. I am only 48 years old. What about my boys? Why is this happening? What is death like? I don't want to be in a coffin under the ground. I'm scared.* Round and round I went through the kitchen into the dining room, into the living room and around again. I walked and walked, thinking and praying and worrying, night after night.

In an effort to cope, I tried to rationalize what was happening to me. I began to organize all my questions and anxiety, and asked myself: *What is the worst that can happen?* The answers eventually started coming to me in a calming and peaceful way, as if someone was giving me the answers that I needed. *The worst that can happen is that I die. I have always believed in things happening for a reason, and I know that if I do die, there will be a reason for it. Maybe it is my time, and maybe that is not so bad. Maybe I am not as good a mother as I think I am. Maybe Mark and the boys will be better off without me. Maybe there are lessons they need to learn from losing their wife and mother. On the other hand, if I do survive, then I know I have a reason to live. Are there things I need to learn from going through this ordeal? Whatever happens is meant to happen.* Eventually I was able to accept the diagnosis and face the challenge, knowing that if I died, all would be as it should be.

Deciding to put my future in the hands of fate loosened the grip of fear and confusion. With a clearer mind, and a more determined attitude, I continued my quest for a course of treatment I could believe in.

I filled my days researching Melanoma drug trials and connecting with others on the Melanoma Patients Information Page (MPIP) online, desperate for something positive to grasp. The message board on this site is, on the one hand a Godsend, and on the other hand, depressing and terrifying. Most postings are from people like me, who were searching for answers and a direction to take. There are also many notices of members who had succumbed to the cancer, after trying every possible option.

On my last visit to my surgeon, he asked if there were anything else he could do for me. I asked him what he thought I should do next, explaining how anxious I was to find a course to take. He replied that I was confused and distraught because, with melanoma there is no right answer. He was sorry, but he had no advice for me. I later realized that what had felt like a dismissal was just the truth about my condition, and I respected that he had been honest with me. Yet I could not accept that this was to be the end of my life. I was not giving up.

I looked into several trials I read about on the Internet, but found only frustration and disappointment. I posted another message on the MPIP, asking if anyone had experience with trials for Stage III melanoma and waited eagerly for any shred of hope. I received many kind and supportive responses with one recurring theme. Several fellow cancer patients and some caregivers recommended that I follow my heart. Choose a path that I felt good about, commit to it, and move forward with a conquering attitude. But where do I find this path?

A fellow San Diegan responded to my post, suggesting I contact the John Wayne Cancer Institute in LA and research their trial. He had also taken part in a trial here at The University of San Diego, which did not work for him, but could be right for me. I immediately made appointments at these relatively close hospitals.

My first appointment was with the director of the Melanoma Care Unit at UCSD. Their trial combined two commonly used chemotherapeutic agents: Cisplatin and Tamoxifen, with the added bonus of Interleuken-2, and Interferon. The thought of ingesting these drugs made me very uneasy, but some encouraging data showed patients disease-free nine years after undergoing this treatment. Dr. McClay, principal investigator of the study and director of the unit, looked over my records and explained the program in a comprehensive and reassuring way. He was upfront about the treatment being difficult to tolerate, but at the same time his confidence gave me hope. He encouraged me to explore all options available before I made my decision. As I walked to my car after that first meeting, deeply engrossed as I absorbed all the new information, a feeling of optimism came over me. For the first time since my diagnosis, I believed I could survive melanoma. This was it! This was a course of action I could feel positive about. I'm not sure what made this decision so clear to me, but I knew this was what I needed to do. However, I had one more trial to investigate.

The following week Mark and I drove to the John Wayne Cancer Institute in Santa Monica, California, to meet with the Medical Director/Surgeon-in-Chief. Through our research, we had learned that this Phase III Randomized Double-Blind Trial of Immunotherapy, plus a melanoma vaccine, CancerVax, looked very promising, and could very well be the light at the end of the melanoma tunnel. The side effects were reported to be minimal. I discovered that a friend of mine worked for the CancerVax Corporation, and the word around her office was that this was going to be a major breakthrough. She strongly recommended that I consider the trial.

Dr. Morton entered the examination room, appearing rushed and flustered. Almost as if it were an inconvenience for him to see me. After a brief description of the trial, he proceeded to direct us toward the registration procedures. But before he could leave the room, I pulled out my list of questions. He did not provide us with any answers, as the study was still in progress, and there was no way to know if I would receive the medicine or the placebo - although, if my cancer did return, I would definitely be given the medicine. *If my cancer returned?* This was not a risk I was willing to take. With his hand on the doorknob, I quickly asked the doctor if he had heard of the work Dr. McClay was doing in San Diego. He said, and I quote: "That's bullshit. There is no evidence that what he is doing has any benefit at all." With that, he left the room. Mark and I were stunned at his blunt and insensitive response. We then listened to the registration nurse describe in more detail the specifics of the study. She understood when I told her I did not think I was going to take part in the trial. I left there feeling sure this was not the right course for me, but with new doubts about the San Diego trial.

At home that night I called my brother-in-law and expressed my confusion and disappointment at the way my appointment with Dr. Morton had gone. He explained to me how frustratingly difficult it is to find eligible patients to participate in trials. He also suggested that this is probably Dr. Morton's life work, and he truly believes the treatment will be hugely successful if he ever gets it approved. Then he encouraged me to follow my instincts, saying also that in his opinion the San Diego trial remained a viable option. Even with my husband by my side, I felt very alone with this decision weighing heavy on my mind.

Why I had such a strong inclination to move forward with a toxic drug cocktail as opposed to a relatively mild vaccine is a mystery. Where does this guidance come from? Is it some otherworldly force or just our own survival instincts? But then, where do these instincts come from? The older I get the more certain I am that we should listen to our *gut feelings,* as more often than not, they are right.

Determined to fight for my life, I scheduled the first of three months of treatments at UCSD. It proved to be far worse than I had ever imagined. I had never tolerated medications or even alcohol very well, and I wondered if I would die from the poisoning drug cocktail, instead of the melanoma. The nausea brought on by the Cisplatin, administered in the hospital, was severe in my case, and I had adverse reactions to the anti-nausea drugs. Following that up at home were daily injections of both Interleuken-2 and Interferon, administered by Mark, which he injected directly into my stomach. My body was being stressed to its limits. It took all the time between treatments for my system to recover enough to hold food down, and then time came to start all over again. If not for the support, encouragement, and care of my husband, sister, mother, and brother-in-law, I would not have completed the trial. They were my strength.

I survived the brutal onslaught, and I am still NED (no evident disease). The five people I connected with on the MPIP all passed away within a couple of months, which makes me wonder why I am still here. Weren't their lives as important as mine? As I watched them leave this world, one after another, I realized how fragile life is, and how temporary.

The advice to follow my heart was good advice, and time has proven my choice was the right one. About four years after I completed my treatment, my friend who worked at CancerVax Corporaton found herself without a job. The vaccine trial I had considered ended in complete failure. To the company's dismay, the patients who got the vaccine did worse than the patients on the placebo.

My journey ended with life, not death. Being diagnosed with melanoma was a difficult and life-changing experience. As many say, once you are faced with accepting your own mortality, every day of life becomes a collection of miracles. Flowers are more fragrant, birdsong is sweeter, and every hug is precious. Was my illness a gift in disguise, or a challenge to build character? Who's to say? What I can say is that my life is now much richer and more meaningful. I find I am at peace with my world, and truly hope that others can find that same inner peace, whatever it takes.

THE CANADIAN ROCKIES

I was so very grateful to be healthy. Even though weak, hairless, and swollen, I was happy. I had my life back. I had my daily routine of getting the boys to their after-school activities, doing laundry, and fixing dinner. Nothing could have been better. I loved every day: Every chore, every errand, every meal, and every restful night. I began to get stronger and healthier with each passing day, and decided I would not miss out on any of life's adventures from that point on. Five months after completing my cancer treatments, Mark and I embarked on a celebratory vacation.

Being lovers of nature and the great outdoors, we chose the Canadian Rockies for our destination. We flew into Calgary, rented a car, and drove towards Banff National Park. We splurged and stayed at the famous "castle" there, and thought we had found heaven. The scenery was spectacular: High forest-covered mountains with waterfalls cascading into jade-colored, glacier-fed rivers and lakes. From our hotel window we viewed the golf course, which more elk populated than golfers. In fact, the elk were everywhere, as well as many other wild animals. We encountered herds of mountain sheep grazing along the highway, momma bears with cubs scampering up the hillside, numerous types of birds, and moose. We could not get enough.

If the castle and town of Banff were heaven, I have no words to describe Lake Louise, our next destination. Again, we treated ourselves to a stay at the beautiful Chateau Lake Louise, with a room overlooking the magnificent lake, which was surrounded by mountains covered with evergreens, emerald green grass, and vivid wildflowers, leading to a glacier at the opposite end of the lake. We donned our hiking boots and set out to conquer the many peaks.

Hiking trails were everywhere. The days were long, and we spent every minute outside. By 7:00 a.m., we had our backpacks loaded, a map in hand, and did not return to the hotel until after 10 p.m., when we lost daylight. I don't know if it was because I had faced death earlier that year, but I was in awe of the beauty of these mountains and lakes. We hiked around the lake to the glacier at the far end and sat gazing at it as it cracked and moaned. This was one of Mark's favorite experiences of the trip. It was late in the day, and we were alone, relaxing on the moraine, almost hypnotized by the silence, the dwarfed, misshapen plants, and the altitude, listening for the glacier to crack. We lost ourselves, and felt as if we were in a dream.

My favorite hike turned out to be one that almost did not happen. I had marked this hike on my trail map, but with so many beautiful trails, we had not been able to fit this one in. The famed Jasper National Park was a few hours north of Lake Louise, and we decided to drive up one day and see as much as we could. We started out early, but were able to get only a taste of the park. The weather threatened to change for the worst, so we decided to return to Lake Louise. The trail I hoped to hike was marked on my map and on the way back, so we planned to take the hike before returning to the chateau.

We arrived at the trail-head as dusk set in, and Mark was against starting out so late in the day. I, on the other hand, really wanted to make the hike. "It is only four miles' roundtrip. We can do it if we hurry along, plus we have flashlights," I encouraged. But he was convinced we could get lost in the dark, die of exposure, or be eaten by bears. Daylight slipped away as I made my case that we just couldn't miss this hike.

During our debate, a car pulled up next to us, and a couple got out and proceeded to prepare for the hike. "Look, that couple is preparing to hike the trail, and they are older than we are. If they can do it, we can certainly do it. If we all hike together, we will be safer." I hopped out of the car to ask if we could join them. They had been having the same discussion - he worried it was too late, and she was unconcerned about the coming darkness. The wives won the argument, and off we went with flashlights and raincoats to discover a glacier only visible from the end of the trail.

The trail was narrow, steep, and winding, but we had just enough daylight and made good time. The higher we got, the smaller the trees and plants got. Exposure to the Canadian Rocky Mountain extreme winter environment limits plants' growing season, and once again knee-high, hobbit-shaped plants surrounded us as we reached our summit. There was no one else around, and a spell was cast on each of us as the late evening light mingled with a swirling mist around our feet. The majestic glacier across the valley shimmered and sparkled in the light of a rising full moon that found its way through the thickening mist, and as if in a trance, we each wandered, alone, exploring this mystical place. The rustle of fat, round ptarmigan, running from bush to bush at our feet, enhanced the peacefulness of the otherworldly aura.

Icy rain pelting my face brought me out of my trance, and I realized the other couple had already started back down the trail. Mark and I rushed to catch up with them. We made our way back to our cars without incident by the light of our flashlights, as the clouds now totally shrouded the moon. As we drove toward our cozy room, the magic of that August night continued as the icy rain turned to snow, dusting everything with a shimmering white powder.

~

We were lucky enough to return to Lake Louise a few years later for a week of skiing with my sister, Julie, and her significant other, Dave. We flew to Calgary, met them there, rented a car, and once again lost ourselves in the beauty of an icy Banff National Park.

The ski conditions were not so great. It had not snowed for the last two weeks, and the slopes were hard-packed and slick. We did ski, but the skiing became secondary to our spectacular surroundings. The weather was clear and very cold, with drifting clouds of frozen fog coating everything with crystalized hoar frost. As it happened, a round, silvery full moon shone down on the lake every night of our stay. Also, as luck would have it, the world ice sculpting championship competition was taking place in front of the chateau. Each evening, after a hearty, hot dinner, we bundled up against the below zero temperature, and ventured outside.

The artists carved magnificent sculptures out of huge blocks of ice, and we checked their progress each night and choose our favorites. The moon illuminated the snow-covered lake and surrounding crystal-covered mountains. A castle built of ice blocks out on the lake added to the fairyland effect. After examining the ice sculptures, we hiked the lake trail surrounded by trees and bushes that glistened and sparkled, reflecting the moonlight, eliminating any need for flashlights, even at midnight. At the far end of the lake, we watched ice climbers scaling a frozen waterfall, where they staked their sleeping bags into the side of the wall of ice and slept.

The moonlit nights at Lake Louise that late February week were pure magic.

~

Mark and Aaron had become certified scuba divers, and keeping with my new attitude to not miss out on life's adventures, Ryan and I accompanied them on a dive trip to Puerto Vallarta. While they spent their days diving somewhere far off shore, we spent ours getting certified, something I never thought I would do. We both successfully passed the course, and on our last day in

Puerto Vallarta, we all experienced the wonders of the deep together.

Over the next few years we took a few more trips centered on diving, including the reefs off Cozumel, and the cenotes; fresh water caves of the Yucatan Peninsula. I had to push myself to complete some of the more challenging dives, but I did it, and I'm proud that I did.

~

While I was still going through my cancer treatments, Mark purchased a house in Escondido, just a few miles north of where we lived. The house was a fixer, and he got it for a reduced price. While I recovered at home, he spent his days working at the fixer, and began to comment on what a nice neighborhood it was, and that the house was turning out really nice. He began to suggest we think about selling our home and moving into it. I was dead set against it. The day I had come to see it before we purchased it, I was nauseous and miserable from the chemo. The dirty, smelly, dark, and unlivable condition of the house, made me feel worse. I could not get past that negative first impression, and could not imagine ever living there. I just wanted my normal life back in my home, with all my belongings in their place.

As I regained my strength, Mark was making major progress on the Escondido house. Finally, I was ready to see why he was so smitten with this property and the transformation blew me away. All the heavy draperies were gone, and the light shone in on the refinished hardwood floors and fresh paint. The new kitchen granite reflected red and green from the colors of the plants beyond the many windows. The landscape had been cleared of years of overgrowth, and the view from the backyard was amazing. *Wow, I thought, this place will sell immediately*. I loved what Mark had done to the property, but not enough to actually move into it. I was still traumatized from my battle with melanoma, Aaron was still in high school, and I just could not face any more disruptions in our lives. Very attracted to the more spacious neighborhood, quiet surroundings, and open view, to his credit Mark did not force the issue, and we put the house up for sale. However, the quick sale I had envisioned was not to be.

On the morning of September 11, 2001, Mark and I woke early, and as usual, he reached for the remote control and turned on the TV. He liked to see what was happening in the world and switched to Mark Haines, (not a typo), the commentator on CNBC, first thing every morning. As we watched and listened to the financial news, Mark Haines interrupted his guest as the camera cut away to the World Trade Center. The commentator was receiving word through his earpiece that a plane had struck the North Tower. Smoke billowed out of a gaping hole in the tower, and as we watched, eyewitness accounts began to come in. A plane had struck the North Tower. At first it was assumed a small plane had accidentally hit the tower, until videos came in showing it to be a large passenger jet. While we watched the stunning video, we witnessed the second passenger airliner fly directly into the South Tower. *Oh my God, this is deliberate.* The nation collectively held its breath. We were stunned, along with all the newscasters, as reality set in that we were under attack. While we dressed for our day, with one ear listening to the news, we knew our country would never be the same.

A cloud of fear and uncertainty settled over the entire country, and the economy stopped as everyone took stock of what was happening, wondering how to move forward. The real estate market came to a standstill, and we wondered how long it would take to sell the Escondido house. After several months of the stalled real estate market, Mark was about to get his wish. With the help of our real estate agent and friend, we surmised a market still existed for the house that we had been living in for twelve years because of its location in an excellent school district, which attracted growing families. Regrettably, I had to agree, but bargained with Mark to do more improvements to the Escondido house before we moved in. He was a good sport about it, knowing I was not keen to move into that house, and made the additional improvements, and then also agreed to put in the vanishing edge swimming pool I envisioned after we were settled.

We made the move, and the following year put in a beautiful pool, totally revamping all the landscape, front and back. We ended up loving the house and our spectacular yard. We have had so much fun over the years with family and our wonderful friends, enjoying the great Southern California weather, barbecuing, swimming, hot tubbing, eating fresh fruits and vegetables from our garden and orchard, that I can't imagine living anywhere else. Mark's instinct was right that this was the place for us, and I am very grateful that we are here. Our home is the go-to place in the summer months for our group of close friends, who have become like family. I wouldn't have it any other way.

MOM

While I was going through my cancer treatments, my mom and sister came when they could to help out, and to give my heroic husband a break. During their visits, my sister and I noticed that Mom was not herself. Granted she had recently lost her husband of fifty years, had had major back surgery, and was watching her daughter endure an onslaught of poisoning chemicals - but still, she was different in some way. Soon after I finished my treatments and began to regain my strength, Mom was diagnosed with Alzheimer's Disease. Another long, heartbreaking journey began for us - a journey that we all knew would not have a happy ending.

My three siblings and I banded together in an effort to keep Mom in her home, sharing her care, and bringing in help as her needs increased. For the first time in our lives, under this tremendous stress, we argued and fought. We all had our own ideas of how best to care for Mom, when in reality there were no right answers. Regrettably, terrible things were said, and our once harmonious relationships were strained. Alzheimer's Disease is the cruelest of illnesses. Over a span of several years, we watched our beautiful, kind, and giving mother forget all of us and retreat into a dark lonely place. Typically, Alzheimer's sufferers can get angry and mean at certain stages, but Mom never lost her sweet nature, even at the worst times. There was never a better, kinder, or more patient mother.

After she passed, the four of us came together for her funeral services. Julie and I went to purchase something pretty for Mom to be buried in. After an hour or so, we both zeroed in on the perfect pink jacket that we knew Mom would have loved and would look beautiful in. After her service, we gathered together at Tedd's house and all the stress, anger, and resentment melted away. By the end of the day, we had made plans to come together once a year for a weekend together. Our reunions continue and are always a lot of fun. After a five-year roller-coaster ride, each of us still bears some scars, but we know we did the best we could. Mom is buried with our dad in the same cemetery as our older brother, Jim, their first-born.

My sweet mother, Beverly Rose Minyard Horbach.

DAVE

David Wayne Haines, DDS, MD, an oral and maxillofacial surgeon, was Mark's youngest brother, of whom he was so very proud. Dave was very successful and highly respected by the medical community of San Francisco, and very much loved by his family and many friends. Despite all of his accomplishments, he was never able to accept his homosexuality, even though he was in a stable relationship and was generally accepted by family and friends for the person he was. He had tried to commit suicide in college, which we did not know about until much later, and unbeknownst to us, he had been self-medicating. As a doctor, he had easy access to drugs, and eventually became an addict.

Two months after we buried my mom, the phone rang one evening. I answered and knew it was going to be bad. David's partner of twenty-years, Virgil, was on the other end, in what seemed to me a hypnotic state. He said that David was dead, and what he had seen was an image that would haunt him forever. The two of them had planned to attend a party that evening, but David was nowhere to be found. The office complex was pretty empty, but Dave's car was still in the parking lot. After checking all around the office, Virgil decided to check the bathroom again. There he found a lifeless Dave, slumped over, with his head against the wall. He called for help, but Dave had been dead for some time, and nothing could be done. Hearing the news, Mark fell to pieces before my eyes. We had no idea Dave had been struggling with drug addiction.

Devastated, Mark and Virgil could not deal with making any of the arrangements, so it all fell to me and Mark's cousins. I had been very close to Dave, also, but put my grieving on hold to rush up to the Bay Area and take care of the business that had to be done. Mark's Italian aunt was adamant about having the funeral in the Catholic Church in the suburbs where we all grew up, even though half of the San Francisco medical and gay communities were rumored to be coming to Dave's services. I wasn't sure how that was going to work out, so we compromised, and had the service at the funeral home with a priest officiating. The chapel held 250 people, so I figured we would be fine. How wrong I was! I think the entire medical and gay communities came out to pay their last respects to our Dave. The chapel filled, and people stood in the aisles and overflowed out the doors. Virgil and Mark remained useless throughout the service, and I barely managed to hold myself together; however, it was a beautiful send-off for this well-loved young man who had never realized what an exceptional person he was.

Dave was laid to rest in the same grave as Mark's and his mother, right next to my brother. It took Mark a long time to get over losing the last and youngest member of his family. I am not sure what would have become of my Mark if I had died also.

The Haines brothers, Mark, Bobby, and Dave.

Chapter 10

JUST US

It was 2:30 in the morning, and I could still hear the boys talking. We were driving Aaron to his dormitory at Chapman University in Orange County early the next morning, and they were still up! I had already told them they needed to get some rest, but it appeared they were as anxious as I was. Exasperated, I got up to reprimand them once again, but stopped outside Aaron's bedroom door, when I heard Ryan consoling his younger brother. Ryan had not gone away to school, having attended The Art Institute of San Diego, earning a degree in advertising while still living at home. As I listened, I could hear Aaron crying, and telling Ryan: "I don't know if I am ready to leave home. What if I fail?"

Ryan replied, "You are going to do great. Do you know how much I wish I could have gone to a university like you are about to go to, and had the true college experience?" With Ryan's encouragement, Aaron began to calm down, and I sensed they were hugging. I did not disturb them and went back to my bed, locking this poignant moment between my two sons away in my heart. It was to be the last night we were all together, living in the same house.

Driving home from Chapman without Aaron after settling him in his dorm room was one of the hardest seventy-mile drives we have ever taken. We both cried the whole way home. We couldn't look in his room for weeks and had to keep his door closed. Just as we got used to Aaron being gone, Ryan began working as a personal trainer and soon moved out also. Suddenly, after twenty-two years of being a family of four, we became empty nesters.

~

It did not take long for us to adjust to the empty nest, and we soon planned a trip to Italy - a trip I had been dreaming about for years. I was slightly anxious about traveling to another continent, leaving the boys behind, but despite my worries, away we went.

ITALY
And
THE ENGLISH PATIENT

It is not surprising that I married into an Italian family. I have always loved everything Italian: the food, the wine, the art, and, of course, my husband. To celebrate our empty nest status and our thirty years of marriage, our dream to experience the glories of Italy had come true. After three magical days wandering the streets and canals of Venice, we were despondent to leave, but excited to be moving on to Florence.

I had never walked so much. The cobblestones were tricky, and the stone floors of the museums are hard on your back. However, I did not want to miss a thing. I woke up on our last morning in Florence, feeling a little out of sorts. *Oh no, I'm not getting sick. I'll just have to buck up and get over it.* We were scheduled to pick up a car and tour the Tuscan countryside. We had reservations for wine tasting at 11:00 a.m. that I didn't want to miss. Mark, being anxious about driving in a foreign country, cringed as horns blared when we pulled out into traffic.

As we navigated the narrow and winding roads of Chianti, I gripped my armrest and struggled with the map, while Mark dodged the competent but aggressive Italian drivers. Determined as I was to shake the nausea I was experiencing, the diesel fumes from our rental, combined with the twists and turns, were getting to me. Still I strained to read the map, but finally had to admit that we may be on the wrong road, and that I was about to lose my breakfast. Mark, white-knuckling the steering wheel quickly pulled off the road, where I emptied the contents of my stomach.

After a little walk and some fresh air, we got back on the road, as I began to feel better. However, the road seemed to be getting worse, with hairpin curves and steep grades. The exhaust fumes seemed stronger than before. Mark was thinking we were still lost. I was getting hot and sweaty, as the nausea returned, but I willed myself to maintain for a few more minutes.

Thankfully we arrived just in time for our wine tasting. It was good to be out of the car as the midday sun warmed the hills and vineyards. The mesmerizing Tuscan light bathed the villa and its gardens in a glow of color. Unfortunately, it was not enough to make me well. Wine tasting was the last thing I wanted to do. Mark drank my samples while I managed to eat some bread and cheese, hoping to settle my stomach.

As we headed to our next destination, I repeated to myself, *I will not be sick, I will not be sick, uh oh, I'm getting sick again. I must fight it off. I am in Tuscany. I can't be sick*. I was having trouble breathing and felt faint. *Breathe, breathe*, I told myself. *What's this? My arms are going numb. Am I having a heart attack?*

I have to get out of this car. " Mark, I'm really sick! Something is happening to me. Pull over. I need help!"

Thinking I was being overly dramatic, Mark looked for a place to pull over. We were in a remote area but saw an establishment up ahead. By then I started to panic. I couldn't catch my breath or feel my arms. "Let me out of this car! I need a doctor."

Mark pulled into the parking area and helped me out of the car. I dropped to my knees on the lawn in front of the car and began to heave. He ran inside and asked for a doctor. The proprietor did not understand much English, but he understood the word "doctor," and he proceeded to make a phone call. A customer, noticing Mark's anxiety and lack of communication skills, offered to translate. "Yes, please," Mark said. "My wife is sick outside, and the gentleman here is looking for a doctor. I am going outside to check on her." The translator followed him and told him there was no doctor in the area, but the proprietor had called an ambulance.

By now I had taken some breaths of fresh air, emptied my stomach again, and was lying on the grass recovering. When Mark returned I told him I was feeling better. He was relieved but exasperated. "There is an ambulance on the way. It's too late for you to be better. Just lie there until they get here." The kind translator offered to stay and help us with the medics. I really didn't want to get back in the car yet, and my arms were numb. *Maybe I should be checked out, I thought.* As I lay in the shade on the grass, I heard a siren off in the distance. *I guess that's for me.*

The ambulance swung into the parking area in a cloud of dust and gravel. Four medics jumped out, all speaking at once, in Italian, and looking for their patient. The translator directed them to me, and two of them rushed towards me while the other two set up a gurney. While the medics checked me over, I tried explaining that I felt better and thought I would be OK. The translator told them my arms had been numb, and they insisted I get in the ambulance. They loaded me onto the gurney and rushed me to the ambulance. In their attempt to slide me into the back, they rammed me into the bumper. They pulled back and rammed me into the bumper again. *What is happening here?* Finally inside the ambulance, where a female medic prepared an EKG, I tried explaining I felt fine, but she didn't understand and proceeded to stick the electrodes onto my chest.

Afterwards she sat beside me, examining the results with a frown on her face. *Oh my God, is something really wrong with me?* Then she started giving directions to the other medics, and it seemed they were preparing to depart, with me still inside.

"Mark, Mark," I called. "What is happening? Have the translator tell them I feel fine!" Mark said the medic saw something she didn't like on the EKG, and they were taking me to the hospital in Florence. "Are you serious? But I feel fine now." Before they shut the back door of the ambulance, Mark said he would follow us back to the hospital.

"Don't lose us! How will you find me if we get separated?" He assured me the driver knew he was following, and he'd see me there. I started to protest again, but the door slammed shut.

I lay back, resigning myself to the situation as the driver forced the ambulance into reverse and backed up at full speed. Making a sharp U-turn on what felt like two wheels, we blasted out of the parking lot. With sirens blaring we raced around curves and bends, while I gripped the sides of the gurney, as I was not even strapped onto it. We entered a small town and sped right through stop signs and stoplights, and I realized there was no way Mark could still be behind us. On his own without his navigator, I feared I would never see him again.

By the time we arrived at the hospital, my heart pounding out of my chest, I had forgotten all about being nauseous. Then it hit me that my purse was in the rental car with Mark. I had no passport, no ID, and no money. "Well, this will be interesting."

The medics escorted me to the registration desk. Of course the receptionist did not speak English and left to get help. Her replacement knew a few words of English, one of them being passport, which, of course, I didn't have, so she went for help.

I waited while the staff discussed in Italian what to do with this English patient. I was taken back to a dormitory-like room with other patients lined up on beds and put on another gurney. Soon a nurse came in to take another EKG, and then left me there alone. I looked down at the other patients, and they seemed content with magazines and visitors. Nobody seemed to notice me. An hour or two went by, and I started fretting about my lost husband. Just as I was wishing he would come walking through the door, a woman from the admissions office came in. Thankfully she spoke some English.

"Where is your passport?" she asked. I tried explaining that my husband had it, and she asked where he was. I told her he should be here soon, not wanting her to know I feared he might never find me. She made some notes, and I asked her about my test results. She explained the doctor would go over them with me, and then left.

I must have dozed off briefly, because I was startled awake by a flurry of activity out in the hall, and heard someone exclaiming: "Ahhh, the English patient." It was Mark! He was at the desk, describing me to the receptionist. She brought him to me, and he was carrying my purse!

He greeted me with a rash of questions. "How are you? What's going on here? Why haven't they released you?" I explained that I had had another EKG, and apparently was fine, because they hadn't felt the need to treat me for anything. I noticed he looked like he had just returned from a war zone and asked where he had been all this time.

"When I saw the ambulance take off like a bat out of hell, I jumped in the car and chased it down. I knew I had to follow closely or I would be lost. I was hanging in there until we came to a roundabout. I was hugging the back of the ambulance, not stopping at the stop signs, when out of nowhere another driver cut in front of me and ran me right off the road. There I was, in a ditch, watching your ambulance disappear from sight. I didn't know how I was going to find you. Once I got up the nerve to get back on the road, I just went in the direction the ambulance had gone. I stopped at a gas station and got the name of the hospital. I didn't understand any of the directions the attendant gave me, but figured I would just keep stopping and asking, now that I had a destination."

"How did you find me? You must have been a nervous wreck."

"You have no idea. As I was leaving one of my stops I saw an ambulance going by with siren and lights flashing, so I jumped out behind it, hoping it would lead me to you, and here I am."

"Thank God you're here. I didn't know what they would do with me with no ID. Our accommodations for tonight are in a remote part of Tuscany, and I have no idea how we will find it in the dark." Neither of us was relishing the idea of more driving. We were feeling pretty disenchanted about the whole trip.

After finally seeing a doctor, we left the hospital with a diagnosis of a virus, which was gone by the next day. We also learned that hyperventilating sometimes causes numbness in the arms. Relieved, we headed back into Tuscany in the dark of night and proceeded to get seriously lost.

We woke up the next morning in a strange hotel, having absolutely no idea where we were. After some time with our maps and a little attitude adjustment, we went on to experience one of the best times of our lives. I would not change a minute of our trip, not even being an English patient for a while.

Me in Tuscany, 2005

~

How wonderful it was to travel without having to worry about kids, and all the extra planning that goes with them. With this new freedom, the travel bug had stung us. I began to watch for travel deals online, knowing that we could now drop everything and go on the spur of the moment. For our next trip we did just that.

Even though we are financially comfortable, we don't spend lavishly, especially on ourselves. So when we went to Italy we flew coach, thinking we would rather put the money towards a longer stay. I did love that trip, except for the long, long flight, in that minuscule seat. I was extremely uncomfortable, suffering from restless leg syndrome, and was not looking forward to enduring another overseas flight in coach, but first or business class seats are so much more money.

While perusing Travelzoo's Top 20 travel deals of the week, I perked up when I saw there was a new all-business-class airline flying to London from Las Vegas. The new airline offered an unbelievably low fare that was too good to pass up. "Mark, do you want to go to London next week?" I asked. He wanted to know the details, and when he heard the price of the business class seats, he was all in. I got busy making the reservations and with the help of our credit card concierge, we planned to take the Chunnel to Paris immediately after landing at London's Stansted Airport. After a week in Paris, we would come back to London for another week before returning home. After a whirlwind of planning, a week later we were at Las Vegas airport for the inaugural flight of the all-business-class MAXjet Airways.

During my adult life I have been plagued with bouts of dizziness - and, at times, been bedridden with vertigo. The morning of our trip I woke up dizzy. Thankfully it was not a severe attack, but just enough to throw me off balance and make me feel nauseous. These episodes usually last about twenty hours. Since I didn't have much choice, I figured if I could just make it to Las Vegas, get on the plane, I could sleep for the eleven- hour flight and would be rested and back to normal when we got there.

I made it to the plane in Vegas, but even with a big comfy chair that leaned all the way back, I still couldn't sleep. Still nauseous, I wasn't able to drink much, so I was getting dehydrated, making matters worse. When we got to London, I was still dizzy and nauseous, but we had reservations on the Chunnel to Paris, so I slugged along. When we emerged from the English Channel, it was dusk, and I could at least enjoy views of the French countryside as we whizzed along towards Paris. I felt horrible, but the thrill of being in France kept me going. When we arrived at the station, Mark found a connection to the Paris Metro (subway), which we had already determined stopped just outside our hotel. The hotel was lovely, and our room was surprisingly large and attractive. "Thank goodness," I sighed, grateful I had survived the journey. I went straight to bed, hoping to be revived for our morning city tour.

I woke up very early, and thankfully was no longer dizzy, but had to go to the bathroom really bad. I got up to pee, and noted that it kind of hurt. I guessed my bladder must have been super full and climbed back in bed. *Wait, what is this pain I am having?* After a few minutes back in bed, I had to go again, and I was in pain. *No, it can't be, not now, not a bladder infection.* But yes, that is exactly what it was. I had all the symptoms, including bleeding and severe pain. *Why, why does this have to happen on our first day in Paris? Now what do I do?* By now Mark was waking up, and I told him I was going down to talk to the concierge about seeing a doctor.

The concierge looked at me a little strangely when I told him I needed to see a doctor right away. I guess in France you don't see doctors *right away*. I told him it was getting to be an emergency, and he told me I would have to go to the emergency room and wait. "I can't wait too long; I am in really bad pain. How long do you think?"

"Several hours, maybe all day," he explained.

"No," I told him. "I need a doctor now." As I clutched my abdomen and doubled over, he discreetly reached under the counter and pulled out a card. He gave me the card and told me it was for a doctor who worked outside of the system for cash payment only. "Fine, I will pay anything. How much do you think it will be?" He didn't know, but he knew it could be very pricey, depending on the services needed. I rushed upstairs to call the doctor, and she said she would be there soon. I sent Mark to the market down the street to get some cranberry juice, and within ten minutes the doctor arrived. She spoke good English and was very professional. She examined me, agreed it was a bladder infection, and prescribed me the necessary medications, including pain pills, and was gone before Mark returned from the corner market. As soon as he got back, I sent him back out to the pharmacy.

Luckily this happened early in the morning, and after another hour in bed, I was up, dressed, and ready to discover Paris. And what a fabulous city it is! We took several educational tours and ate the best food of our lives. Then it was back to London for another amazing week with glorious fall colors and an unusually warm sun. For a trip put together in a week, it was fantastic.

THE BEST TRAVEL COMPANIONS

By now we were becoming seasoned travelers. On a trip to Oregon to visit our close friends from Alaska, Paul and Patti, Patti and I devised a trip to Italy for the four of us to celebrate her 50th birthday. We had a blast. They love Italy as much as we do. The following year, Mark and I returned for a third Italian vacation and will definitely go again. It is our favorite destination.

For our next European adventure, we decided to try a river cruise. We had heard how fantastic they were and had to agree the television ads made them look wonderful. It would be just the two of us. Most of our friends still worked, or couldn't afford to travel internationally, so I began planning a month-long extensive trip beginning in Prague, Czech Republic, joining Uniworld River Cruises there, and continuing for a week cruising the Danube River through Austria, ending in Budapest, Hungry. After touring Budapest we would fly to Munich, Germany, pick up a car, and explore Germany; including the German and Austrian Alps.

I worked for months planning this trip, every hotel, every tour, our driving routes, and even restaurants. Nothing was left to chance, and it was going to be the trip of our lifetime. All the household bills were paid, the mail stopped, Aaron would check on the house regularly, and I was proud of the work I had put into this amazing trip. Finally, it was the evening before our early morning departure. Everything was ready except for receiving one last confirmation for our tours of Prague. We closed our suitcases, put them in the foyer, and planned to retire early. I just had to check for that last tour confirmation that should have arrived in my email.

Yes, I got it. Now my travel documents will be complete. I opened the email and read, "We are sorry to inform you that your tours of Prague have been canceled due to the flooding."

Flooding? I thought. *What flooding*? I did a quick Google search of flooding in Prague, and learned that our entire itinerary was underwater, or about to be underwater, as the rivers, including the Danube, overflowed their banks and flooded many of the towns we were planning to visit. Our flight was to land in Prague the next day, which I read had no functioning power or sewer system. I began to panic. Mark was at the store getting last minute items, so I tried to call the travel agent I had used to book the cruise portion, and luckily she was working late.

"Sonja, what are you hearing about the flooding in Germany?" I asked.

"Flooding, what flooding? I haven't heard about any flooding."

I told her about our tour cancellation and what I had seen online. She said she would call Uniworld and get right back to me. In the meantime, Mark came back and I explained to him what was going on. He got on his computer, and we learned that the flooding was getting worse. Pictures were coming in of people standing in hip-high water. We didn't know what to think. We just sat there waiting for Sonja to call back. Finally, the phone rang.

"Bad news," she said. "Your cruise and your hotel reservations in Prague have been canceled. The river is too high, and Uniworld cannot operate their cruises."

We were stunned. Our efficiently packed suitcases sat by the door, and we already had our boarding passes. The flights were still going as scheduled, but we didn't think we wanted to fly into a flood zone. I made a heroic attempt to plan something else, but it was just not to be. We were so disappointed, but decided we would put the trip on hold until sometime in the near future.

What a letdown, after all my planning and preparations, there would be no trip. It took us a couple of days to face unpacking our suitcases. We moped about the house for a couple of days since our calendars were clear for the trip, and all of our friends thought we were out of town. River cruising is so popular that I was not able to get us on another Uniworld River Cruise until the following October, which was four long months away. The rescheduled cruise was of the Rhine and Mosel rivers, starting in Basel, Switzerland, ending in Amsterdam, so I had to rearrange our entire trip.

Sometimes things happen for a reason. Since we had to join our cruise in Basel, we flew into Paris (mainly for the food), rented a car and drove around France heading east through Burgundy towards Switzerland. There really were no large towns along our route, so we stayed in small towns and villages, including the

Medieval village of Noyers. This centuries-old village is frozen in time, and we loved, loved, loved it. There was a total of two choices for accommodations, both Bed & Breakfast establishments.

October is very "off season" in France outside of Paris. We toured the Chateau of the Loire Valley, without encountering any other tourists, and when we arrived at our accommodations in Noyers, there was no one there, not even the proprietress. We knocked at the ancient wooden gate with the large metal knocker, but received no reply. After dark, there was not a soul to be seen anywhere in the village. Finally, we heard the locks from inside clang open and were greeted by a smiling, bubbly young woman with an *English* accent! She explained that the owner had been called away on a family emergency, and that she, Jenny, would be taking care of us. We entered through the gates into a courtyard surrounded by a centuries-old residence, with the towers of the village church looming behind it, casting long, eerie shadows. Jenny showed us our room, gave us the keys to the front gates, and told us she would be back in the morning to serve us our breakfast, and then disappeared out the gate. Left alone in the dark, shadowy courtyard, dwarfed by the tall medieval buildings, gave us both the shivers. I wondered how many ghosts lurked in the shadows as Mark locked the gates, and we made our way to our room with the flashlight Jenny had left us when, suddenly, the church bells gonged, scaring the wits out of us.

We spent an uneasy night snuggled together, listening to the rain, in that spooky old house from the Middle Ages. By morning the sun was shining and we found Jenny in the main house with a cheery smile, coffee, and fresh croissants. Jenny was from Australia. After surviving cancer she decided to leave her life there as a banker. She sold her properties, and come to Noyers to live permanently. She purchased an eight hundred-year-old house, restored it, and lives happily among the village residents. We became great friends and she gave us a tour around the area, including a tour of her fantastic home with the original eight hundred-year-old stone floors and beamed ceilings. We met many of the locals, and the entire time we were treated as special guests. We spent three nights there, staying alone at the B&B, and thankfully did not encounter a single ghost.

The last stop on our way to Basil was at an elegantly restored hunting lodge, built in the 1700s for the Marquis de Germigney. The lodge is set in the most beautiful surroundings, and learning of our love of nature and history, our hostess directed us to some of the most stunning villages on the surrounding hilltops, and on our last day to the unique and spectacular Source of the Lison. The Lison River literally comes out of the side of the mountain in the form of waterfalls, spouts, and rivers. We spent the entire day, once again the only tourists to be seen, exploring and marveling at this unique and mesmerizing natural water park.

As amazing as our time in France was, the best part of this trip was yet to come. We finally arrived in Basel, dropped our car at the airport, and had a taxi drive us to the dock where the Uniworld River Queen prepared to launch at 6:00 p.m. Our twelve days on the River Queen were filled with touring French and German towns and villages, and then meeting back on board for the evening. We found ourselves joining a certain group of people for dinner each night because we all hit it off, having a great time together. Three of them were from Portland, Oregon, and another couple hailed from Oakland, CA. Even though we had never met, and came from different backgrounds, we enjoyed each other's company so much that we began to tour together, meeting for dinner every night, having our waiter set our table for seven. By the end of the cruise, we were great friends and decided to book another cruise, as a group, the following year. We have already been on four trips together, and have three more in the works.

Enjoying wine and great food at a dinner in Berlin on one of our trips, someone remarked at what a stroke of luck it was that we were all on that first river cruise together. Mark interjected that we were not supposed to be on that cruise, and it was only because our Danube River cruise was canceled that we were on it at all. One of the other couples mentioned that they were only on it because their travel plans had changed also. It turns out it was fate that brought us all together. And now we enjoy the easiest, classiest (except for Mark and I), most fun people to share our travel adventures with. We would never have met them if our first trip had not been canceled.

~

Mark and I continued skiing together for a few years after the kids moved out, but after I turned sixty, I began to be less enthusiastic. In addition to not wanting to injure myself again, it had just lost its thrill for me. Luckily Mark has a friend to ski with, and that takes the pressure off of me. When Mark is gone skiing, I watch chick flicks on our big screen television, get together with my girlfriends, and don't worry about, "What's for dinner?"

MARK LEARNS TO USE A GO-PRO

As members of the aging baby-boomer generation, we are generally not as savvy as our children and grandchildren when it comes to the latest technological gadgets. When Mark announced he was finally going to experience one of his life-long goals, and had booked himself for a week of helicopter skiing in the Canadian Rockies, none of the family was too surprised. Being dropped off at the top of an otherwise inaccessible mountain in the dead of winter, for the first time at the age of sixty-three, may seem extreme to some people, but if you knew my husband, you would shrug and look forward to the stories of his exploits upon his return.

As Christmas approached, Aaron, who is an amateur photographer, decided his dad needed a GoPro camera, the type of video camera you strap to your helmet, for his upcoming ski trip. I agreed it would be the perfect gift, so that Mark could capture the experience from his perspective, and then share it with us once he returned home safely. He was delighted to receive such a great gift when he opened it on Christmas morning.

In preparation for the extreme skiing in Canada, Mark had planned to go skiing locally to work on his form and get in shape. He also wanted to learn to use the GoPro so he would be sure to get some great shots of this once-in-a-life-time adventure. He read the instructions, secured the camera to his helmet, and headed to Mammoth Mountain with his friend for some fun on the snow.

After a day or two of getting some good practice on the slopes, Mark decided to focus on using the camera. His companion took the afternoon off, so as Mark began each ski run, he would reach up and turn the camera on as he headed down the mountain. When he reached the bottom, he would reach up and switch it off. The camera is made for this easy on/off operation, but not being able to see the switch, it took a little getting used to. The thick, awkward ski gloves didn't help either, but he seemed to be doing fine and assumed he was capturing some great footage of his afternoon runs.

After Mark returned home, the day came to figure out how to get the videos from the camera to the television screen. I suggested he wait for one of the boys to come by to help, but he didn't want to wait and set to work connecting the camera to his laptop computer, and then the computer to the television. The process took time, many expletives, and some frayed nerves, but lo and behold, there on our big screen TV we could watch the tips of Mark's skis schussing down the slopes as pretty as could be. We watched together and marveled at the technology that allowed us to sit in our family room and almost feel the wind on our faces, as if we were skiing the run together. After viewing a few videos, Mark put one on for me and left to answer a phone call.

I was enjoying the scenery rushing by and felt as if I were skiing myself, when Mark reached the bottom of the run, skied up to the lodge, and reached up to turn off the camera. His hand came down, but the camera was still on. He proceeded to take off his skis, put them in the rack, apparently thinking the camera was off. I watched as he climbed the stairs to the lodge, kicking the snow off his ski boots, pushed the door open, and headed inside. I got a view of the skiers at the bar having a beer, and when he turned his head I saw the restaurant filled with people eating lunch, and then, oh no, he is heading for the bathroom! *Mark,* I thought, *You didn't go in there with that camera on!* But yes, that is exactly what he did. Then there it was, on the TV screen, the door of the men's room, being pushed open and a wide view of the interior came into view. The camera scanned back and forth as Mark looked for a vacant urinal, capturing the backs of the other users as they stood at the urinals and other men as they secured their belts and zipped jackets on their way out. By this time, I was in hysterics. This was just so typical of the kind of antic my husband is known for, and as he assumed his position at a vacated urinal, with the camera still filming, I thought I would die laughing. I couldn't see him, but the image of him sauntering into the men's room with that camera secured to his head, with the red "camera on" light blinking was just too much.

My laughter brought Mark back into the family room, wondering what could be so funny on his ski films, until he looked at the TV, exclaiming "What's this?"

"It's you in the men's rooms at Mammoth with the GoPro on," I stammered through my hilarity as we watched his urine stream arc into the toilet bowl.

"But I turned the camera off, or at least I thought I did," he stated, as he sat down to watch.

He had no idea the camera was on when he went into the bathroom, and after I rewound the video we watched, rolling with laughter, as he innocently scanned around the bathroom filming the unsuspecting skiers taking their bathroom break.

Mark returned home from his helicopter ski trip in one piece and with some great shots from the peaks of the Canadian Rookies. I was a little disappointed after watching the films, though, as there was not a single bathroom shot. Life with Mark is never boring.

~

Life continues to rain blessings on us. The four of us are healthy. The boys are finding their way in the world and live locally, so we see them regularly. Early retirement is allowing us to pursue interests that during our working/child-rearing years there was not time for. We both exercise regularly and eat well to stay healthy and fit for our travels. When we are not on a trip, Mark keeps busy managing our rental properties, our fruit trees and garden, and our money. I indulge myself in my favorite past-times, reading lots of books, writing, and I have become a CASA, (Court Appointed Special Advocate) for foster children. As a court appointed volunteer, I monitor all aspects of my assigned *case child* and become the eyes and ears of the judge, who only sees the child at court hearings. I submit an in-depth report to the judge before each court hearing, and this is his/her best overview of how the child is doing. I hope I can make a difference in at least one child's life.

I am continuing to learn as I travel my life path. At our yearly family reunions, I have learned that my parents grew our 'family' by welcoming and caring for friends of my siblings who did not have a stable home. Jon, my brother Jim's best friend, was basically abandoned by his parents and left to fend for himself in his home at the age of fifteen or sixteen. When my parents were made aware of his situation, they took care of him as if he were one of their own. Jon was always with us, having meals, and sleeping over. At the time, I did not realize that my parents had taken him in. Jim passed away all those years ago, but Jon remains a brother to us, and we see him at all family get-togethers. I have heard other friends of my brothers' tell the stories of how my dad guided them towards success in life, when they had no one else to guide them. Now, when we have family gatherings, including the kids my parents took under their wings, I marvel at the wonderful gift they left for their four surviving children, lifelong friends, that truly are our family.

GOING FORWARD

Mark and I feel so lucky to have found our traveling companions. They have traveled extensively, and we are benefiting from their experience. As much as we love to experience new things, we also enjoy being homebodies. We love to get comfy in our family room and watch football or movies on our big screen TV. When the weather is fine, which is much of the year for us, we love to set up our lounge chairs in our resort-style backyard and enjoy our view and sparkling swimming pool. If not for Linda, the main travel planner of our group, we certainly would not have three major trips already on our calendar. These adventurers do not let any grass grow under their feet before they are looking to the next great journey. As soon as we return from one trip, and sometimes while still traveling, they are planning for what is next. It can be overwhelming for us, but like the saying goes, be careful what you wish for. We wished we knew people that we liked, who were easy to travel with, and had the time and money to do it. Well, we found these people on that first river cruise in Germany, and so we are putting our reservations aside and committing to exotic trips to Indonesia, India, and Africa. Soon we will be off to Greece and Croatia as well. Following these trips, we will visit Sicily and Southern Italy, not to forget the parts of the United States we have yet to discover. Seeing at least some of each of our fifty states is on my bucket list.

Life has turned out pretty well for a baby girl born in Richmond, California, in 1953. It has not always been easy, but it has been rich, and rewarding. Every experience, even the difficult ones, has made me who I am today. Did I make some bad choices? Yes. Could I have been a better parent? Yes. Have I been charitable enough? Probably not, but I am still learning and will be until the day I die. At sixty-three I am learning to let go, to be less judgmental, and to free myself of all the things I worry about. Worrying does not fix anything. I am striving to live the next chapter of my life peacefully, and with grace and humility. I hope my golden years are truly golden.

www.ingramcontent.com/pod-product-compliance
Lightning Source LLC
Chambersburg PA
CBHW060018100426
42740CB00010B/1518

* 9 7 8 1 9 3 7 5 0 8 5 4 8 *